CONSTRUCTION METHODOLOGIES

& PROCEDURES FOR CIVIL ENGINEERS

PART -1

TALLA BALRAM BALAKRISHNA

BlueRose ONE.com
Stories Matter
NewDelhi • London

BLUEROSE PUBLISHERS
India | U.K.

BlueRose ONE.com
Stories Matter
NewDelhi • London

For permissions requests or inquiries regarding this publication,
please contact:

BLUEROSE PUBLISHERS
www.BlueRoseONE.com
info@bluerosepublishers.com
+91 8882 898 898
+4407342408967

ISBN: 978-93-6261-297-7

Cover Design: Sadhna Kumari
Typesetting: Pooja Sharma

First Edition: May 2024

The information provided in this book is just for guidance and it needs to be customised as per your project and material requirement.

FOREWORD

"Procedures & Methodologies for Construction Engineers", this book is designed to be an indispensable companion for construction/practicing engineers, providing a comprehensive guide to the various procedures and methodologies essential for success in the field. The procedures and methodologies given in this book are very much appropriate and can be easily implemented on the sites during construction.

Construction engineering is a dynamic and multifaceted discipline that requires a deep understanding of sequencing of various construction activities, technical principles, project management techniques and regulatory frameworks. From the initial planning stages to the final execution of a project, construction engineers play a vital role in ensuring that structures are built safely, efficiently and within budget.

In this book, a wealth of information covering extensive topics, including surveying, excavation, formwork, reinforcement, concreting, masonry works, plastering, painting, Mivan works, VDF Flooring, Tile flooring, painting etc, each topic is carefully written to provide practical insights, sequencing of construction activities that would empower construction/practicing engineers to tackle challenges with confidence and expertise.

For a seasoned professional or a student just starting the journey in construction engineering, this book is intended to serve as a valuable resource that will enhance the knowledge, skills and capabilities. It is my hope that the information contained within these pages would inspire us to strive for excellence in the work and make meaningful contributions to the advancement of the construction industry.

I extend my heartfelt gratitude to **Sri. Talla Balram Balakrishna** who has shared his expertise and experiences to make this book possible. His dedication and commitment to the field of construction engineering are truly commendable.

The procedures and methodologies outlined in this book, I encourage readers to approach each topic with an open mind and a spirit of curiosity. Embrace the challenges, seek out new opportunities for growth and never stop learning. "Success is a result of doing it right the first time and never settling for less"

We are very much thankful to you to produce the book "Procedures & Methodologies for construction engineers – Part 1. You have given absolute important sequencing of various construction activities and other information in this book, we cannot express our happiness in words and therefore just say thanks to produce the above book.

Together, let us strive to build a future where innovation and excellence define the landscape of construction engineering.

Best wishes.

Dr. Venkat Praveen Gannavaram

Professor & Head

Department of Civil Engineering

Sreenidhi Institute of Science and Technology, Hyderabad

CONTENTS

1. METHODOLOGY FOR SURVEYING 1
2. METHODOLOGY FOR EXCAVATION 4
3. METHODOLOGY FOR PLAIN CEMENT CONCRETE 7
4. METHODOLOGY FOR PLUM CONCRETE 10
5. METHODOLOGY FOR ANTI TERMITE TREATMENT 13
6. METHODOLOGY FOR FOOTINGS 16
7. METHODOLOGY FOR BACKFILLING 19
8. METHODOLOGY FOR RCC FOR STARTERS, COLUMNS, BEAMS & SLABS 22
9. METHODOLOGY FOR BLOCK WORK 33
10. METHODOLOGY FOR INTERNAL PLASTERING 38
11. METHODOLOGY FORMS RAILING WORK FOR SIT- OUT / BALCONY / UTILITY / CORRIDOR / OUT DOOR UNIT 42
12. METHODOLOGY FORMS RAILING WORK FOR STAIRCASE 46
13. METHODOLOGY FOR EXTERNAL PLASTERING 48
14. METHODOLOGY FOR WATERPROOFING WORKS- TOILET / UTILITY / SIT-OUT / BALCONY 52
15. METHODOLOGY FOR WATERPROOFING WORK -TERRACE 56
16. METHODOLOGY FOR WATERPROOFING WORKS FOR PODIUM, RETAINING WALL, SWIMMING POOL, STP, UG SUMP, FIRE SUMP, GRADE SLAB & LIFT PITS 59
17. METHODOLOGY FOR KITCHEN PLATFORMWORK 62
18. METHODOLOGY FOR TILING WORK - DADO 65
19. METHODOLOGY FOR TILING WORK - FLOORING 69
20. METHODOLOGY FOR TILE DADO WORK – KITCHEN / WASH BASIN 74
21. METHODOLOGY FOR FIXING OF UPVCWINDOWS /DOORS 77
22. METHODOLOGY FOR FIXING OF ALUMINIUM VENTILATORS 81
23. METHODOLOGY FOR FIXING OF DOOR FRAMES 84

24. METHODOLOGY FOR FIXING OF DOOR SHUTTERS 87
25. METHODOLOGY FOR TANDUR FLOORING - STAIRCASE 90
26. METHODOLOGY FOR INTERNAL PAINTING WORKS 94
27. METHODOLOGY FOR EXTERNAL PAINTING WORK 98
28. METHODOLOGY FOR VACUUM DEWATERED FLOORING 101
29. METHODOLOGY FOR SCREED WORK 105
30. METHODOLOGY FOR RUBBLE SOLING WORK 108
31. METHODOLOGY FOR STONE MASONRY WORK 110
32. METHODOLOGY FOR EXPANSION JOINT TREATMENT 113
33. METHODOLOGY FOR FIXING OF MS DOOR / ALUMINIUM LOUVER FOR SHAFTS 116
34. METHODOLOGY FOR TOILET FALSE CEILING WORK 119
35. METHODOLOGY FOR GRANITE / MARBLE WORK - LIFT LOBBY - FLOORING 122
36. METHODOLOGY FOR GRANITE / MARBLE – LIFT CLADDING 128
37. METHODOLOGY FOR SWIMMING POOL WORKS 133
38. METHODOLOGY FOR MIVAN STRUCTURE 136
39. METHODOLOGY FOR GYPSUM PLASTERING WORKS (MIVAN STRUCTURE) 148
40. METHODOLOGY FOR INTERNAL PAINTING WORK (MIVAN STRUCTURE) 153

01

METHODOLOGY FOR SURVEYING

1. Scope:

- This method provides a system of control for **"Surveying"** in order to accomplish compliance with the specifications and drawings.

2. Drawing Reference:

- Footing Layout/ Column Layout/ Shuttering Layout/ Block Layout Drawing/ Floor Plans/ Relevant Drawing if any.

3. Equipment's:

- Total Station with accessories, laser machine & Auto Level with accessories.

4. Tradesman:

- Surveyor & Helpers.

5. Work Policy:

5.1. Construction of marking pillars at every 50 meters should be done for traversing for the whole site.

5.2. Block corner pillars construction should be done for checking of block set-backs.

5.3. Block column grid pillars construction should be done in X and Y directions, at a distance of 2 meters from the block boundary.

5.4. Footings should be casted by grid wise either in X-direction or Y-direction.

5.5. At the time of plinth beam casting, column size should increase all-round by 50mm for further column markings.

5.6. For plinth beam survey, at least 10 columns should be casted.

5.7. After slab concreting, slab surface & flat sunken areas housekeeping should be done.

5.8. Reinforcement steel should not be shifted to slab before marking.

5.9. 1 meter marking should be given by the surveyor over the column in each floor.

6. Methodology:

6.1. Column marking (3 corners) should be given over PCC surface. According to column grid drawing, column marking and column distance should be checked by means of steel tape by site team along with the surveyor. After confirmation, block in-charge should sign in the check list.

6.2. After pedestal casting, column starter marking (3 corners) should be given by surveyor and block in-charge should cross check with the GFC drawing.

6.3. Column marking (3 corners) should be given over plinth beam. Block in-charge should cross check for column marking and column distance with GFC drawing and after confirmation he should sign in the check list.

6.4. After slab casting, flat corner column/wall plumb should be checked with reference to below floor column/wall starter.

6.5. For conventional structure, Column marking (3 corners) should be given over slab, column to column measurement should be cross checked by block in-charge using floor plans/ GFC drawings.

6.6. After surveyor marking, block in-charge should cross check with floor plans /GFC drawings and after confirmation he should sign in check list.

7. Quality Control & Quality Assurance:

7.1. Ensure approved drawings are available before start of Survey work

7.2. Work policies are to be monitored and are to be strictly implemented in site.

7.3. Check for dimensions & levels of foundation pit.

7.4. Check for top levels of PCC.

7.5. Check for slab top levels of concrete and ensure levels are within tolerance.

7.6. Check for Deviation survey [verticality checking of the structure for every five floors.

8. Safety:

8.1. Safety PPE's will be provided for workers.

8.2. First aid box will be provided at the site office.

9. Miscellaneous:

9.1 For any mismatches in Arch & Structural drawings, immediately highlight to Project Manager before proceeding.

02

METHODOLOGY FOR EXCAVATION

1. Scope:

➢ This method provides a system of control for **"Excavation"** in order to accomplish compliance with the specifications and drawings.

2. Drawing Reference:

➢ Footing Layout/ Block Layout Drawing.

3. Equipment's:

➢ Total Station with accessories, Excavator / JCB, Dumpers, Breaker and other tools if any etc.

4. Tradesman:

➢ Operator's & Drivers, etc.

5. Work Policy:

5.1. Gridline and measurements of the trench/ foundation must be checked with respect to the final good for construction (GFC) drawing. Working space should be provided as per requirement/IS-1200.

5.2. All loose earth, roots of plants/ trees, inorganic matter etc. must be removed.

5.3. Masonry pillars should be erected at suitable points in the area to serve as bench marks.

6. Methodology:

6.1. RL of bottom of pit foundation must be checked with respect to the GFC drawing.

6.2. Measurements of foundation pit should be checked before proceeding to the next activity.

6.3. For more excavation depths, adequate side slope/ berms must be considered to retain the sides.

6.4. Any kind of water flooding near the pit is to be avoided.

6.5. Prior to execution ensure that all bench marks such as NGL (Natural Ground Level), FFL (Finished Floor Level), etc. should be taken out on some permanent structures for reference during construction.

6.6. Control blasting must be done for boulders/ sheet rock if necessary.

6.7. Proper care should be taken to dump the excavated earth away from the edge of excavation.

7.Quality Control & Quality Assurance:

7.1. Ensure approved Quality checklist is available before start of excavation work

7.2. Trial pits to be taken for soil/ rock classification.

7.3. Work policies are to be monitored and are to be strictly implemented at site.

7.4. Check for dimensions & levels of foundation pit.

7.5. Submit soil samples in third party laboratory for MDD (Maximum Dry Density) & OMC (Optimum Moisture Content).

8.Safety:

8.1. Safety PPE's will be provided for workers.

8.2. First aid box will be provided at the site office.

8.3. Proper barricading, shoring, shuttering must be provided for safety wherever required.

9.Miscellaneous:

9.1 For any mismatches in Arch & Structural drawings, immediately highlight to Project Manager before proceeding.

03

METHODOLOGY FOR PLAIN CEMENT CONCRETE

1. Scope:

➢ This process provides a system of control for **"Plain Cement Concrete for Footings & Grade Slab"** work in order to attain compliance with the specifications and drawings.

2. Drawing Reference:

➢ Footing Layout / Floor Plan Drawing (Architectural & Structural drawings).

3. Equipment's:

➢ Auto Level with accessories, RMC Plant/ Concrete Mixer, Transit Mixer, Needle Vibrator, Straight Edge, etc.

4. Tradesman:

- Operators, Driver, Carpenter, Masons & helpers.

5. Work Policy:

5.1. Make sure that dewatering must be done prior to concrete pour and the area must be kept dry till initial setting of concrete.

5.2. Make sure that the excavated/ back filled formation level should be free from loose material and well compacted to required field density.

5.3. Reduced levels of minimum 5 nos. must be recorded for the bottom of PCC for the footing.

5.4. Reduced levels at regular intervals must be recorded for the bottom of PCC for grade slab.

5.5. Make sure anti termite treatment - stage-1 has been done at bottom of PCC for footing as per work order.

5.6. Ensure a trench has been provided for services prior to PCC for grade slab as per relevant drawing.

5.7. Make sure anti termite treatment - stage-3 has been done at bottom of PCC for grade slab as per work order.

5.8. Measurements, level & centre line of the footing must be checked prior to concreting.

5.9. Shuttering height, straightness, alignment and cleanliness should be checked prior to concreting.

5.10. Working condition of mixture machine, vibrators and other tools must be checked prior to concreting.

5.11. Care must be taken to sprinkle water and ram in foundation pit before placing concrete.

6. Methodology:

6.1. Diagonal check must be done and proper bracing should be provided.

6.2. Check to be done for mix proportion of concrete as specified.

6.3. Check to be done for placement and proper compaction of the concrete to the required level and top level must be checked.

6.4. Check for protection of the concrete surface.

6.5. Ensure curing for minimum 7 days.

7. Quality Control & Quality Assurance:

7.1. Ensure approved Quality checklist is available before start of PCC work.

7.2. Cement, Fine Aggregates, Coarse Aggregates, Water, Fly ash & Chemical Admixtures should be conforming to relevant standards.

7.3. Work policies are to be monitored and are to be strictly implemented at site.

7.4. Sampling of concrete cubes for 7 days& 28 days compressive strength.

7.5. Ensure the compressive strength of 7 days & 28 days as specified.

7.6. Check for top levels of concrete.

7.7. Ensure curing for minimum 7 days.

8. Safety:

8.1. Safety PPE's will be provided for workers.

8.2. First aid box will be provided at the site office.

9. Miscellaneous:

9.1 For any mismatches in Arch & Structural drawings, immediately highlight to Project Manager before proceeding.

04

METHODOLOGY FOR PLUM CONCRETE

1.Scope:

- This method provides a system of control for **"Plum Concrete Work"** in order to attain compliance with the specifications and drawings.

2.Drawing Reference:

- Footing Layout Drawing/ Relevant Drawing.

3.Equipment's:

- ➢ Auto Level with accessories, RMC Plant / Concrete Mixer, Transit Mixer, Steel / Wooden Rammer, Straight Edge, etc.

4.Tradesman:

- Operators, Driver, Masons & helpers.

5. Work Policy:

5.1. Excavated formation level should be cleaned and free from loose material.

5.2. Top level of plum concrete should be marked.

5.3. Ensure proper reinforced anchorage if the plum is to be laid on rock.

5.4. If the height of plum concrete is more than 750mm, consultant approval has to be taken.

6. Methodology:

6.1. Depth must be divided into layers of 300mm.

6.2. Volume of plum concrete required for 300mm layer must be calculated.

6.3. Stone boulders are to be collected in between 150mm to 200mm size equal to 70% / 50% of above volume.

6.4. Pour concrete of M 7.5 / M 10 grade equal to 70% / 50% of volume calculated in step 6.2, intermittently keeping all the stone collected as above.

6.5. Concrete to be compacted properly with steel / wooden rammer.

6.6. Steps 6.1 to 6.3 are to be repeated till the required level is attained.

6.7. Curing should be done as per the normal construction practice.

7. Quality Control & Quality Assurance:

7.1. Ensure approved Quality checklist is available before start of plum concrete work

7.2. Cement, Fine Aggregates, Coarse Aggregates, Water, Mineral Admixtures & Chemical Admixtures should be conforming to relevant standards.

7.3. Work policies are to be monitored and are to be strictly implemented at site.

8.Safety:

8.1. Safety PPE's will be provided for workers.

8.2. First aid box will be provided at the site office.

9.Miscellaneous:

9.1 For any mismatches in Arch & Structural drawings, immediately highlight to Project Manager before proceeding.

05

METHODOLOGY FOR ANTI TERMITE TREATMENT

1. Scope:

- This method provides a system of control for **"Anti Termite Treatment"** work in order to attain compliance with the specifications and drawings.

2. Drawing Reference:

- Footing Layout Drawing/ Relevant Drawing.

3. Equipment's:

- Sprayer, mixing tools, etc.

4. Tradesman:

- Competent and experienced person from anti-termite agency.

5. Work Policy:

5.1. Confirm that proper compaction of the soil prior to treatment. And the soil should be ready for laying PCC below the grade slab.

5.2. Ensure to compare soil compaction with respect to Maximum Dry density and optimum moisture content.

5.3. Confirm that the soil surface should be dry prior to treatment and treatment should not be carried out when it is raining or the soil is saturated.

5.4. Work methodology to be submitted by the vendor and to be approved by PMC

5.5. Mockup to be done prior to start of work as per the material specification

5.6. Check lists to be maintained & PMC should certify the work done prior to payment to contractor in phase wise.

5.7. Only approved skilled person is allowed to do the entire phase of work

6. Methodology:

6.1. Confirm that the chemical must have proper shelf life.

6.2. 1part of Chlorpyriphos must be diluted with 19 parts of water or as per work order to get the required emulsion for application.

6.3. Anti termite treatment has to be done as per the approved method statement of that particular applicator.

6.4. Application of anti termite treatment for Stage-1: Treat the sides and bottom surface of the pits and foundation trenches with chemical to a height of about 300mm at the rate of 5 lire per square meter of surface area or as per work order.

6.5. Application of anti termite treatment for Stage-2: Backfill earth on each side of all built up walls, which will be in immediate contact with the foundation, should be treated with chemical at the rate of 7.5 liter per square meter of vertical surface of the sub-structure, to a depth of 450mm and width of 150mm or as per work order.

6.6. Spray chemical must be directed towards concrete surface.

6.7. Application of anti termite treatment for Stage-3: Before laying the floor, treat the top surface of the consolidated earth within the plinth walls with chemical at the rate of 5 liter per square meter. Ensure back fill against foundation is treated to its full depth or as per work order.

6.8. Concrete must be allowed only after drying of treated surface.

7.Quality Control & Quality Assurance:

7.1. Ensure approved Quality checklist is available before start of Anti Termite treatment work

7.2. Chemical should be conformed to relevant standards.

7.3. Ensure the chemical dilution & dosage rate for application has been done as per manufacturer's recommendations.

7.4. Work policies are to be monitored and are to be strictly implemented at site.

8.Safety:

8.1. Protective clothing such as apron, face mask, hand gloves, shoes, etc. shall be provided.

8.2. First aid box will be provided at the site office.

06

METHODOLOGY FOR FOOTINGS

1. Scope:

➢ This method provides a system of control for **"RCC Footing / Stepped Footing/ Simple Spread Footing / Slopped Footing / Combined Footing Works"** in order to achieve compliance with the specifications and drawings.

2. Drawing Reference:

➢ Footing Layout / Relevant Drawing.

3. Equipment's:

➢ Total Station / Auto Level with accessories, Steel cutting & bending machine, RMC Plant/ Concrete Mixer, Transit Mixer, Needle Vibrator, Straight Edge, Measuring tape, etc.

4. Tradesman:

➢ Operators, Driver, Carpenters, Bar-benders, Masons & helpers.

5. Work Policy:

5.1. Contactor's Engineer should call PMC/Quality Engineer for prior permission for a group of footings/pedestals of minimum 10nos/as required.

5.2. PCC top levels should be cross checked after proper cleaning of mud/soil if any over the surface.

5.3. Anchor reinforcement from PCC/plum concrete should be extended up to footing top mat with development length.

5.4. No overlapping of column reinforcement should be allowed at footing level.

5.5. Column stirrups have to be tied up to plinth beam level before concreting of footing.

5.6. Adequate support should be provided for verticality of column reinforcement.

5.7. PMC/Quality Engineer should check for column center line marking, footing dimensions, footing/column/pedestal reinforcement, and cover prior to approval as per the drawings

5.8. Shuttering should be provided only after reinforcement checks done by PMC/Quality Engineer.

5.9. Plinth beam/pedestal top level to be marked over column reinforcement prior to concrete.

5.10. Pedestal height should not be more than 3 times least lateral dimension/if it is check with the design consultant before proceeding.

6. Methodology:

6.1. Slope should be checked as per specification for sloped footing.

6.2. Check should be done for the availability of vibrator, proper cleaning, grade of concrete, Cement slurry pouring prior to concrete etc.

6.3. Shear keys should be provided for bonding of upper level concrete.

6.4. Broom finishing & curing should be done as per methodology.

6.5. Footing concrete has to be completed within 24 hours of approval from PMC/Quality Engineer, if failed checking is void and fresh checking should be requested again.

7. Quality Control & Quality Assurance:

7.1. Ensure approved Quality checklist is available before start of RCC Footing work

7.2. Cement, Fine Aggregates, Coarse Aggregates, Water, Mineral Admixtures & Chemical Admixtures should be confirming to the relevant standards. Ensure approved mix design & proper grade of concrete has been used.

7.3. Work policies are to be monitored and are to be strictly implemented in site.

7.4. Sampling of concrete cubes to be done for 7 days & 28 days compressive strength.Slump test to be conducted at site.

7.5. Ensure that the compressive strength of concrete for 7 days & 28 days has been achieved as specified. If any failure inform Project Manager.

7.6. Ensure that de-shuttering has been done within 16 to 24 hours/As per IS 456.

7.7. Ensure that curing has been done for minimum 10 days.

8.Safety:

8.1. Safety PPE's will be provided for workers and First aid box will be provided at the site office.

8.2. Proper illumination to be provided for night work. For footing concreting, barricading will be provided at sides.

9.Miscellaneous:

9.1 For any mismatches in Arch & Structural drawings, immediately highlight to Project Manager before proceeding.

07

METHODOLOGY FOR BACKFILLING

1. Scope:

- This method provides a system of control for **"Backfilling"** work in order to achieve compliance with the specifications and drawings.

2. Drawing Reference:

- Footing Layout Drawing and relevant drawing.

3. Equipment's:

- Excavator / JCB, Dumpers, Water Tanker, Power Roller – 8 to 10 MT, Field Compaction Testing Equipment's, etc.

4. Tradesman:

- ➢ Skilled worker, Operator's & Drivers, etc.

5. Work Policy:

5.1. Ensure that the earth used for filling shall be of approved quality team, free from salt, organic or other deleterious matter.

5.2. PMC/Quality Engineer clearance must be taken prior to backfilling of earth retaining and water retaining structures where waterproofing treatment is there.

6. Methodology:

6.1. All lumps and clods exceeding 80mm must be broken.

6.2. Backfilling or filling in plinth / trenches must be done in layers of maximum 300mm thickness.

6.3. Backfilled soil should not be allowed to fall on top of brick masonry / concrete members, etc. However, once it falls, that should be cleaned / washed thoroughly.

6.4. Each layer is to be properly spread, watered and compacted. Ramming / compaction should be done by suitable equipment preferably by mechanical rollers.

6.5. Compaction must be carried out with 8 to 10MT power rollers.

6.6. Consolidation of filling must be done up to 95% of density at optimum moisture content and is to be ensured for each and every layer.

6.7. Proper care must be taken to ram near walls, columns and plinth beam sides in layers of 300mm thickness properly.

6.8. Ensure that the consolidated top layer must be dressed to required slope and level.

7.Quality Control & Quality Assurance:

7.1. Ensure approved Quality checklist is available before start of Back filling work

7.2. Backfilling Soil should be conforming to relevant standards.

7.3. Work policy to be monitored and are to be strictly implemented at site.

7.4. Check for Field Compaction Test and ensure the 95% of compaction is achieved as specified.

8.Safety:

8.1. Safety PPE's will be provided for workers and First aid box will be provided at the site office.

08

METHODOLOGY FOR RCC FOR STARTERS, COLUMNS, BEAMS & SLABS

1. Scope:

- This procedure provides a method of control for **"Reinforced Cement Concrete Works"** in order to achieve compliance with the specifications and drawings. The topics covered in this documents are mentioned below:

1) Starters/kicker for Columns/ Core Wall.

2) Reinforcement for Column / Core Wall.

3) Formwork for Columns / Core Wall.

4) Concrete for Columns / Core Wall.

5) Formwork for Slab and Beams.

6) Reinforcement for Slab and Beams.

7) Concrete for Slab and Beams.

2. Drawing Reference:

- Column Layout / Schedule Drawing, Shuttering Layout Drawing, Structural Drawings & BBS.

3. Equipment's:

- Total Station / Auto Level with accessories, Steel cutting & bending machine, RMC Plant/ Concrete Mixer, Transit Mixer, Needle Vibrator, Straight Edge, Measuring tape, etc.

4. Tradesman:

- Operators, Driver, Carpenters, Bar-bender, Masons & helpers.

5. Inspection Request Policy: Inspection request should be continued in the specified format and should reach the concerned PMC/Quality engineer by 9.30 AM on the same day or by evening for the next day planned works. Prior to PMC/Quality Engineer inspection, vendor/contractor/Client engineer inspection must be completed. Inspection request should specify area of work to be inspected viz. starter of columns, columns, slab & beams, lifts walls, staircase etc. One-day prior notice to the consultants should be given for their check and clearance.

Drawing copies available at site should be latest. BBS should be kept ready for prior checking. For dimensions and geometrics architecture drawings will take precedence over structural drawings.

6. Starter / Kicker for Columns/ Core Walls:

6.1. Work Policy:

6.1.1. Contractor's Engineer should call PMC/Quality Engineer for minimum one flat after doing marking for columns/Core wall starter, PMC/Quality engineer should check for room dimension, column/Core wall reinforcement, and covers and give approval flat wise.

6.1.2. Column/Core wall ring has to be tied after approval of starter marking and before concreting.

6.1.3. Lapping for the column/Core wall reinforcement has to be done prior to starter concreting to avoid damage to the starter while lapping.

6.1.4. Starter concreting has to be completed within 3 hours of approval from PMC/Quality Engineer, if failed checking is void and fresh checking to be requested again. Site mix concrete may also be used for concreting.

6.1.5. After 6 PM starter concreting is not allowed, PMC/Quality Engineer should be more vigilant on this aspect.

6.1.6. Before calling for inspection for checking of marking of starter, contractor engineer should ensure proper cleaning of the slab concrete. All loose mortar and debris should be thoroughly cleaned.

6.1.7. No cranks shall be allowed in the column, if any then structural consultant's opinion should be taken. To accommodate electrical conduit properly, 40mm cover has to be provided.

6.1.8. All the end columns/Core wall should be checked for verticality with the below floor by using plumb.

6.2. Methodology:

6.2.1. Ensure proper shear keys between Slab-Starter and Starter –Column/Core wall.

6.2.2. If starters are permitted with site mix, then supervisor should be present at batching plant and PMC/Quality Engineer should check for the approved mix design of the concrete.

6.2.3. Post concrete check will be done for all starters with emphasis on dimensional check of the room.

6.2.4. Starter offset not to be more than 2mm.

7. Reinforcement for Columns/ Core Wall:

7.1. Work Policy:

7.1.1. After contractor/client engineer checking of all columns/ Core wall in one flat, PMC's/Quallity Engineer's inspection will be called for.

7.1.2. Column/ Core wall reinforcement tying permission will not be given if no staggering of laps provided.

7.1.3. Structural drawings should be followed strictly.

7.1.4. Ensure usage of approved binding wire for tying reinforcement.

7.1.5. Contractor before calling for steel checking should ensure for tying of cover blocks for the main reinforcement along the height

7.1.6. For Columns: Laps will not be permitted at beam junction. Welding if required to avoid laps in junction will be carried upon structural consultant's advice.

7.1.7. For Columns: Wherever there is increase in number of bars, the additional bar should have development length from the bottom of the slab.

7.1.8. For electrical/services points, clearance from MEP team should be taken.

7.2. Methodology:

7.2.1. Reinforcement should be checked as per drawing for diameter of bar, spacing and laps. Lap length shall be provided as per drawing.

7.2.2. Check for the reduction of the column if any, the spacing of stirrups should be half of the actual spacing for the reduction portion.

7.2.3. When bars of two different diameters are to be spliced, the lap length shall be calculated on the basis of diameter of the smaller bar.

7.2.4. Electrical points if any will be provided in the columns and concurrence to be taken from MEP site team.

7.2.5. Stirrups up to 1m height above next slab level to be tied.

8. Formwork for Columns / Core Wall:

8.1. Work Policy:

8.1.1. Number of repetitions will be checked, any rejected material not to be used at site.

8.1.2. If column box/ shuttering is used for first time, dimension check should be done.

8.1.3. Tie rods must be provided at regular intervals.

8.1.4. Staging should be provided for each column.

8.1.5. For columns in expansion joint, both columns should not be casted at the same time but one after other with a gap of one or two days.

8.1.6. Beam bottom level should be clearly marked on column box.

8.1.7. For inspected and approved columns/core wall, concreting should be done on the same day, if not inspection should be done again.

8.2. Methodology:

8.2.1. Dimensions and alignment of boards are to be checked prior to placing of formwork.

8.2.2. Formwork ply boards should be cleaned and thoroughly applied with shuttering oil.

Check for previous repetitions.

8.2.3. Check for the plumb.

8.2.4. Electrical points to be sealed properly to prevent entry of concrete.

8.2.5. Battens or walers to be provided as additional support.

8.2.6. Props to be provided all round the column

8.2.7. Foam sheets should be provided to prevent slurry leakages.

8.2.8. Alignment of columns with the adjacent columns to be checked at the top level.

8.2.9. Ensure proper cover for the column reinforcement.

9. Concrete for Columns/ Core Wall:

9.1. Work Policy:

9.1.1. Slump test, incoming timings, grade of concrete, temperature checks for the concrete will be done at site quality lab.

9.1.2. Contractor's Engineer should order for correct grade of concrete as per drawing, if SMC then PMC/Quality engineer will check batching before concrete starts

9.1.3. Water should not be added to concrete for increasing workability, admixture to be used.

9.1.4. All end columns should be checked for verticality with below floor.

9.1.5. Post pour check will be done for columns/ core walls.

9.1.6. Columns plumb deviation should not be more than 3mm per 3m height.

9.1.7. Severe honeycomb with steel exposure should be treated with approved method statement from consultant.

9.1.8. Column caps of more than 200mm should not be allowed.

9.2. Methodology:

9.2.1. Ensure proper platform for the column / core wall concreting.

9.2.2. Cement slurry has to be poured into the starter before pouring concrete.

9.2.3. Concrete to be poured in layers and each layer has to be compacted properly by using needle vibrator.

9.2.4. Concrete to be poured up to the bottom of the beam as marked on the column reinforcement.

9.2.5. Shear keys have to be provided after initial concrete set.

9.2.6. Post pour concrete will be checked for plumb and level.

10. Formwork for Slabs and Beams:

10.1. Work Policy:

10.1.1. Architectural drawing should be strictly followed for Formwork.

10.1.2. Level marking on columns to be done at 1m height from existing slab top.

Shuttering height will be transferred and checked from the 1m marking for slab/beam bottom. Surveyor will provide level at one point per floor and this has to be transferred to the required locations.

10.1.3. Shuttering to be checked in stage wise. Contactor engineer will call for checking as follows:

1st - Beam bottom: Alignment, level and rigidity of staging to take the load.

2nd-Beam sides, room dimensions

3rd - Slab Shuttering and levels, Sunken slab depth for toilets/Utility/ Sit-out and balcony projections

4th - Fixing of side supports etc. for rigidity after reinforcement.

10.1.4. For Balconies, cantilever slabs and for staircase mid landing cup lock system must be used.

10.1.5. Tie rod should be provided for all the peripheral beams and for internal beams of more than 450mm depth side supports to be provided.

10.1.6. External elements, balcony and sit-out elevation drawings to be referred in addition to floor plan.

10.2. Methodology:

10.2.1. Special care should be taken to check column caps, supports at junction of beams. C clamps should be provided for the column caps.

10.2.2. At construction joints C clamps to be provided for beam bottom immediately after the joint on both sides.

10.2.3. Slab levels will be checked along with dimensions for the rooms as per drawings.

All External beam and columns will be checked for plumb with respect below floor.

10.2.4. Cutouts, sunken slab will be checked as per architectural and services drawings.

10.2.5. For MEP services like cutouts, sleeves, approvals will be given by MEP engineer.

10.2.6. Podium Slab de-shuttering should be done only after 21 days, and re-propping should be done immediately and retained up to 28 days.

11. Reinforcement for Slab and Beams:

11.1. Work Policy:

11.1.1. Structural drawings will be followed strictly for all reinforcement details of slabs and beams

11.1.2. Bar bending schedule should be available at site prior to reinforcement work commences however the slab reinforcement will be checked as per structural drawings.

11.1.3. Ensure usage of approved binding wire for tying reinforcement.

11.1.4. Reinforcement for the beam to be checked before downing of the beam reinforcement.

11.1.5. If any dowels to be left, they should be staggered for both the beam and slab with development length.

11.1.6. Recheck should be done for the dimensions after lowering of beam reinforcement.

11.1.7. Lockset if any has to be done, PMC/Quality Engineer approval must be taken prior to start of the work.

11.2. Methodology:

11.2.1. Cover to be checked for the beam bottom, sides and end sections.

11.2.2. Check reinforcement for size, spacing, location, numbers, lap length, development length, hooks and ties as per drawings and bar bending schedule for slab.

11.2.3. Chairs of 12mm diameter to be provided adequately for slab.

11.2.4. Spacer bars to be used between 2 layers of reinforcements in beams (minimum diameter of spacer is 25mm).

11.2.5. Ensure that the stirrups to be tied properly at the column beam junction.

11.2.6. The projected beam dowels should be tied with at least one stirrup to avoid disturbance to the reinforcement. The length of the bar in the slab should be equivalent to Ld.

11.2.7. No personnel movement should be allowed on the reinforcement, if required planks, floor plates are to be provided as walkways.

12. Concrete for Slabs and Beams:

12.1. Work Policy:

12.1.1. All construction joints to be identified and clearance to be taken before casting.

12.1.2. For concreting at construction joints old concrete to be chipped and cleaning to be done, and epoxy bonding agent must be applied over the joint.

12.1.3. The concrete shall be poured up to the marked level.

12.1.4. After initial setting a the same time the concrete in grey condition broom finish to be done to avoid shrinkage cracks.

12.1.5. Post pour concrete check will be done for slab casted for level, undulations flat wise, beam side bulge.

12.1.6. No cement will be allowed to be spread on slab at low levels where slurry is accumulated. For beam alignment, ±3mm sideways, bottom and visible deflection will be allowed.

For slab top level up to ± 6mm level to be allowed.

For dimensions of column/beam a variation of +10mm & -5mm shall be allowed

12.2. Methodology:

12.2.1.1. First columns should be casted with stoppers up to 200 mm from column edge and up to slab top with the specified grade of concrete.

12.2.1.2. The sunken areas to be concreted first and the others areas to be concreted after completion of the sunken areas.

12.2.2. Concrete should be compacted properly by using needle vibrator.

12.2.3. The Concrete should not be stacked beyond the height of 300 mm at one place.

12.2.4. Concrete surfaces should be finished with broom.

12.2.4.1. Vehicular movement should not be allowed over podium slab up to 28 days after concreting.

13. Quality Control & Quality Assurance:

13.1.1. Cement, Fine Aggregates, Coarse Aggregates, Water, Mineral Admixtures& Chemical Admixtures should be conform to relevant standards. Ensure approved mix design& proper grade of concrete has been used.

13.1.2. Steel should be conform to relevant standards.

13.1.3. Work policies are to be monitored and are to be strictly implemented at site.

13.1.4. Sampling of concrete cubes for 7 days& 28 days compressive strength & Slump test to be conducted at site.

13.1.5. Ensure the compressive strength of concrete cubes for 7 days & 28 days has been achieved as specified.

13.1.6. Check for slab top levels of concrete and ensure levels are within tolerance.

13.1.7. Ensure curing for minimum 10days (for podium slabs minimum 14 days by ponding).

13.1.8. Ensure de-shuttering has been done after confirmation of 67% of 7 days cube compressive strength has been achieved/ As per IS: 456 – 2000.

14. Safety:

14.1.1. Safety PPE's will be provided for workers. First aid box will be provided at the site office.

14.1.2. Proper lighting to be provided for night work. For slab concreting, barricading will be provided at sides.

09

METHODOLOGY FOR BLOCK WORK

1. Scope:

- This method provides a system of control for **"Block Work – Walls"** in order to attain compliance with the specifications and drawings.

2. Drawing Reference:

- Floor Plan / Block Layout Drawings / Furniture Layout / Relevant Drawings.

3. Equipment's:

- Trowel, Mixing Platform, Mixer machine / spade, Measuring Box, Water Drum, Plumb Bob, Aluminum Straight edge, Sprit level, Square ruler, Tube level, line-dory, Measuring tape, etc.

4. Tradesman:

- Masons & helpers.

5. Inspection Request Policy: Inspection request will be continued in the format as it is and to be submitted to the concerned PMC/Quality engineer by 9.30 A.M.

Contractor/Client engineer inspection to be completed before PMC/Quality Engineer inspection. Inspection request shall specify area location of work to be inspected.

6. Work Policy:

6.1. Structure checklist must be closed prior to commencement of block work.

6.2. Architecture drawings are to be referred for layout dimensions. Refer furniture layout plan for door locations & services drawings for service locations.

6.3. Drawing copies available at site should be latest.

6.4. All honeycombs and leakages should be treated. Tapes, nails, ply stuck and foam sheets shall be removed prior to commencement of block work.

6.5. All sunken shall be cleaned and loose concrete in ducts shall be removed and broken edges of sunken shall be treated.

6.6. All steel rods used for starters and safety aspects shall be cut to level before starting of block work.

6.7. All concrete surfaces shall be hacked (50 to 60 nos. per SFT), debris and dead mortar shall be removed.

6.8. 1 m level marking from SSL, should be given on lift wall in corridor and this has to be referred for levels in each flat. Levels to be marked on the column for lintel level, sill level.

6.9. All tie rods holes in the columns/ beams shall be closed with non-shrink grout.

6.10. Avoid stacking of blocks over the slabs at one place.

6.11. Work should be started only upon prior intimation to PMC/Quality engineer, Un- intimated works will not be allowed.

6.12. Site engineer should check for the outer/peripheral dimensions after layout is laid and then check internal wall as per latest architecture drawing. Plumb to be checked with respect to outer beams and block work to be marked accordingly. Also for higher floors, plumb of the outer wall to be checked with reference to the lower floor.

6.13. First layer of block work to be done for minimum of 2 Flats prior to calling for the inspection. Ensure that no broken or edge chipped off blocks should be used in the first layer of block work.

6.14. Dry mortar will be mixed in plant and carried to work place, where water will be added and consumed within 30 minutes to 1 hour.

6.15. For door openings 32 mm on either side and for windows 25 mm all around block work should be left to accommodate plaster, foam and sealant. For Main door 35mmgap to be left all around or you may leave the place as per the respective project requirement.

6.16. DPC should be laid at window sill level.

6.17. Chasing for electrical conduits shall start only after curing for a minimum period of 7 days and proper marking must be done prior to chasing.

6.18. For Toilet/ 100mm thick walls chasing for services will be done only after one coat of rough plaster.

6.19. Block work to be completed in 2 levels below prior to take up the third level.

6.20. Block work for external architectural elements should start simultaneously with the block work of flats and to be completed in the span of 3 floors.

6.21. Date of completion of block work above lintel to be marked on walls.

6.22. Curing shall be done for a minimum period of 7 days on internal and external faces.

6.23. Mockup has to be done for every block and has to be approved.

7. Methodology:

7.1. DPC layer shall be provided on periphery& partition walls for 50 mm thick.

7.2. Blocks shall be made wet prior to the laying.

7.3. All the RCC surfaces must be coated with cement slurry for better bonding.

7.4. All openings and corners shall be checked for right angles at various levels for uniformity.

7.5. All the joints should be of uniform thickness of 10mm. Joints to be raked for good bonding for plastering.

7.6. Block course height shall not raise more than 1m per day.

7.7. For 100 mm walls RCC bands shall be provided at every 5^{th}layer with 2nos of 8 mm steel with M 15 concrete.

7.8. Vertical joints must be staggered.

7.9. Bearing for lintels, sill and chajjas should not be less than 200 mm/ as per drawing.

7.10. For block course under roof beam, if the gap is more than 15 mm, concrete screed has to be laid at bottom of the layer and full block has to be placed at the top layer and is to be properly packed.

8. Quality Control & Quality Assurance:

8.1. Ensure approved Quality checklist is available before start of Block work

8.2. Cement concrete blocks, Cement, Fine Aggregates should be conforming to relevant standards. Ensure ratio of mortar mix is used as specified.

8.3. Work policies are to be monitored and are to be strictly implemented at site.

8.4. Ensure DPC layer has been provided on periphery& partition walls for 50 mm thick.

8.5. Ensure all the joints are uniform thickness of 10mm and joints are raked.

8.6. Ensure for 100 mm walls RCC bands are provided at every 5^{th}layer.

8.7. Ensure bearing for lintels, sill and chajjas are provided not less than 200 mm/ as per drawing.

8.8. Check for line, plumb, right angle, room dimensions, and window& door openings.

9. Safety:

9.1. Safety PPE's will be provided for workers.

9.2. First aid box will be provided at the site office and good housekeeping will be ensured.

9.3. Proper platform will be made for wall height.

10

METHODOLOGY FOR INTERNAL PLASTERING

1. Scope:

- This method provides a system of control for **"Internal Plastering for Walls and Ceilings"** in order to achieve compliance with the specifications and drawings.

2. Drawing Reference:

- Floor Plan / Block Layout Drawings/ Relevant Drawings.

3. Equipment's:

- Trowel, Mixing Platform, Measuring Box, Mixer machine / Spade, Water Drum, Plumb Bob, Aluminum Straight edge, Template, Sprit level, Square ruler, Tube level, line-dory, Measuring tape, etc.

4. Tradesman:

- Masons & helpers.

5. Work Policy:

5.1. Prior to start of plastering works, Block work shall be cured for 7 days & post checklists must be closed.

5.2. Before plastering all the lintels must be casted.

5.3. All debris shall be removed and cleaned for centerline marking.

5.4. Before starting of plastering all the external beam holes and any extra openings should be closed with non-shrink grout and curing for 3 days.

5.5. Bull marks for minimum of 1 entire flat to be done before calling the PMC/Quality Engineer for checking. Ceiling plaster and wall plaster to be done preferably by same mason and should happen simultaneously to avoid the undulations in the corners.

5.6. Bull Marking to be done for wall & ceiling at a time. If any chipping is required permission from PMC/Quality Engineer to be obtained as all the services has to be coordinated.

5.7. MEP clearance must be taken prior to plastering.

5.8. Electrical switch boxes must be filled with sand prior to plastering.

5.9. Plastering is not allowed if the upper floor block work is incomplete.

<u>5.10. Top floor plastering to be done only after completion of terrace water proofing.</u>

5.11. GI mesh of 18 gauges has to be provided for all junctions between the concrete and masonry surfaces, plastered and cured for 2 days in advance.

5.12. Glass fibers are to be used for the top two floors by mixing them with mortar as per the manufacturer specifications.

5.13. GI mesh has to be placed diagonally for door and window openings at all corners for 300mm length and 150mm width.

5.14. All the wall chases should be closed with mortar and GI mesh specified and cured for 3 days before start of plaster for walls and in coordination of services like electrical and plumbing.

5.15. Internal plastering thickness is up to 20 mm (25 mm for top two floors) in cement mortar (1:6) and Ceiling plaster thickness is up to 12 mm in cement mortar (1:4).

5.16. Skirting portion to be checked for line and level and a gap of 200 mm to be left out above SSL without plaster for skirting/ or refer and execute as per architectural drawing.

5.17. If plastering has gone up to 3rd floor, ensure plastering checklists must be closed in the lower floors.

5.18. Date of completion of plaster must be marked on the plastered surface.

5.19. Curing should be done for a minimum period of 7 days.

5.20. Proper lighting to be provided during the work, if required.

5.21. Mockup has to be done for every block and has to be approved.

6. Methodology:

6.1. Centre line / Reference line should be taken from the corridor and line perpendicular to the center line to be taken into the flats.

6.2. Centre line and offset line for each room shall be marked and Bull marking shall be done with reference to this offset line.

6.3. Sufficient bull marks should be made available

6.4. All the bulged beams should be chipped off in line with the plastering bull marks.

6.5. GI Mesh of 200 mm of 18 gauges should be fixed rigidly at all junctions between concrete and masonry and 150 mm for electrical chasings.

6.6. Ensure that 1 meter level markings are made available on all walls.

6.7. All surfaces should be made sufficiently wet prior to commencement of plastering.

6.8. Cement mortar mixed should be consumed within 1 hour after adding water.

6.9. Undulations in plastered walls to be checked with aluminum straight edge and line dori. If any undulations, it should be rectified immediately while the plaster is fresh.

6.10. Spilled mortar on Electrical junction boxes, on walls should be cleared on the same day of work.

6.11. All door and window openings after plastering should be checked by templates as per specification.

6.12. Day to day plastering work dead mortar shall be removed and proper housekeeping to be maintained at site. Excess water in the floors and sunken to be removed on regular basis.

7. Quality Control & Quality Assurance:

7.1. Ensure approved Quality checklist is available before start of internal plastering work

7.2. Cement, Fine Aggregates should be conforming to relevant standards. Ensure ratio of mortar mix and thickness of plaster is used as specified.

7.3. Check for line, plumb, right angle, room dimensions, and window / door openings.

7.4. Work policies are to be monitored and are to be strictly implemented at site.

8. Safety:

8.1. Safety PPE's will be provided for workers.

8.2. First aid box will be provided at the site office and good housekeeping will be ensured.

8.3. Proper platform to be made for wall height and ceiling.

11

METHODOLOGY FORMS RAILING WORK FOR SIT-OUT / BALCONY / UTILITY / CORRIDOR / OUT DOOR UNIT

1. Scope:

- This method provides a system of control for **"MS Railing Work for Sit-out / Balcony/ Utility / Corridor / Out Door Unit"** in order to attain compliance with the specifications and drawings.

2. Drawing Reference:

- Floor Plan / Architectural Drawings / Relevant Drawings.

3. Equipment's:

- Drilling machine, Welding machine, Grinding machine, Plumb Bob, Sprit level, Square ruler, Line-dory, Measuring tape, etc.

4. Tradesman:

- MS Railing Fixing Contractor & workers.

5. Work Policy:

5.1. Block work must be completed prior to start of railing work.

5.2. One meter marking above SSL must be ensured floor wise prior to fixing of railing.

5.3. For conventional structure: Sit-out/ balcony / utility areas railing fixing should be done with reference of external plastering bull marks. For MIVAN structure, Sit-out / utility /ODU railing fixing should be done with reference of internal wall plaster/ bull marks.

5.4. Gaps must be provided in the block work prior to fixing of railing to avoid chippings.

5.5. All the dimensions of the railing members must be checked at the fabrication yard only as per the given specifications/drawings.

5.6. All railings have to be checked by PMC/Quality Engineer & site engineer for bends, right angles, weld joints, grinding for weld joints, any dents, end caps etc. before shifting only.

5.7. Zinc chromate/as specified in BOQ, primer has to be applied at fabrication yard only prior to shifting.

5.8. Mockup should be done for every block and has to be approved.

6. Methodology:

6.1. Railings have to be shifted according to the elevation drawings only to avoid unnecessary stacking and damage due to re shifting.

6.2. All railings in a particular face in all flats have to be fixed to the horizontal and vertical alignments.

6.3. All the railings have to be fixed as per the given levels before external plastering only.

6.4. Anchors to be provided to the R.C.C. columns & beams for proper fixing/welding to the railings.

6.5. Gaps provided in the block work for fixing of railings must be filled up with concrete and ensure that legs are also firmly fixed in the concrete.

6.6. Uniform gap has to be maintained at both the ends of the utility and corridor railings as per the drawings and end caps are to be fixed.

6.7. For balcony, sit out & outdoor unit railings, bottom rail to ledge gap should be uniform.

6.8. For any missed gaps of railing joints, metal putty must be applied.

6.9. After railing fixing, it should be properly protected.

6.10. Two coats of approved paint to be applied along with second coat of internal painting

7. Quality Control & Quality Assurance:

7.1. Ensure approved Quality checklist is available before start of MS railing works at Sit out, Utility, Corridor and ODU.

7.2.

7.3. Work policies are to be monitored and are to be strictly implemented at site.

7.4. Check for line, level, plumb, right angle and dimensions.

8. Safety:

8.1. Safety PPE's will be provided for workers.

8.2. First aid box will be provided at the site office and good housekeeping will be ensured.

12

METHODOLOGY FORMS RAILING WORK FOR STAIRCASE

1. Scope:

➢ This method provides a system of control for "MS Railing Work for Staircase" in order to attain compliance with the specifications and drawings.

2. Drawing Reference:

➢ Floor Plan / Architectural Drawings.

3. Equipment's:

➢ Drilling machine, Welding machine, Grinding machine, Plumb Bob, Sprit level, Square ruler, Line-dory, Measuring tape, etc.

4. Tradesman:

➢ MS Railing Fixing Contractor & workers.

5. Work Policy:

5.1. Tandur works must be completed earlier to start of staircase railing.

5.2. Plastering for walls, waist slab ceiling and sides must be completed prior to start of staircase railing.

5.3. All the dimensions of the railing members must be checked at the fabrication yard only as per the given specifications/drawings.

5.4. Mockup should be done for every building and has to be approved.

6. Methodology:

6.1. Check must be done for drilling of holes in the tandur and anchor bolts with MS plate is to be provided before hand rail fixing.

6.2. Check should be done for vertical members to be fixed first and then horizontal members and check for line, level & alignment of all members.

6.3. Check to be done for equal gap between edge of tandur and vertical rail.

6.4. All railings have to be checked for bends, weld joints, grinding for welded joints, any dents etc.

6.5. Check must be done for application of primer.

6.6. Check must be done for application of two coats of approved paint.

7. Quality Control & Quality Assurance:

7.1. Ensure approved Quality checklist is available before start of MS railing work at stair case.

7.2. Work policies are to be monitored and are to be strictly implemented at site.

7.3. Check for line, level, plumb, right angle and dimensions.

8. Safety:

8.1. Safety PPE's will be provided for workers.

8.2. First aid box will be provided at the site office and good housekeeping will be ensured.

13

METHODOLOGY FOR EXTERNAL PLASTERING

1. Scope:

- This method provides a system of control for "External Plastering for Walls" in order to attain compliance with the specifications and drawings.

2. Drawing Reference:

- Elevation / Architectural Drawings / Relevant Drawings.

3. Equipment's:

- Trowel, Sprit level, Mixing Platform, Measuring Box, Water Drum, Mixer machine / Spade, Plumb Bob, Aluminum Straight edge, Square ruler, line-dory, etc.

4. Tradesman:

- Masons & helpers.

5. Work Policy:

5.1. Block work must be completed and cured for 7 days prior to plastering works.

5.2. Lintel and chajjas must be casted prior to plastering.

5.3. Proper scaffolding should be erected for external plastering work.

5.4. Bull marks of entire face from ground floor to terrace must be done before calling the PMC/Quality Engineer for checking.

5.5. GI mesh of 18 gauges has to be provided for all junctions between the concrete and masonry surfaces and cured for 2 days in advance.

5.6. All external railings shall be fixed prior to commencement of plastering work in that particular elevation.

5.7. Column & beam tie rod holes shall be grouted & all exposed steel bars to be cut prior to plastering.

5.8. All the bulged beams should be rectified in line with the external plastering bull marks.

5.9. Ensure that all RCC surfaces must be properly hacked.

6. Methodology:

6.1. All surfaces should be made sufficiently wet prior to commencement of plastering.

6.2. Plastering shall be carried out band wise and unless it is completed, work in the next band shall not be taken up.

6.3. Cement mortar mixed should be consumed within 1 hour of adding water.

6.4. External Plastering thickness is up to 25 mm in cement mortar (1:4) in two coats with waterproofing compound, lintel and sunshades plastering thickness is15 mm in cement mortar (1:4).

6.5. All external grooves (25mm wide x 12mm deep) shall be marked on surface of plaster after 1st coat to ensure proper depth or as per architectural drawings.

6.6. For external plastering in two coats, the first coat shall be cured for minimum 3 days and then second coat shall be started and ensure that the surface must be wet prior to start of second coat plastering.

6.7. Undulations in plastered walls shall be checked with aluminum straight edge and line dory. It should be rectified immediately while the plaster is fresh.

6.8. Chajjas, sit out, balcony, plumbing duct & elevation fins plastering alignment must be checked with line dory and any misalignments should be rectified immediately.

6.9. Water drip moulds (12mm wide x 8mm depth) shall be provided for sunshades and sit outs or refer architectural drawings.

6.10. All window jambs must be matched with the internal plastering.

6.11. Window sill plastering should be sloped outside.

6.12. All window openings after plastering should be checked with templates.

6.13. Date of completion of plastering shall be marked on the surface.

6.14. Curing should be done for a minimum period of 7 days.

7. Quality Control & Quality Assurance:

7.1. Ensure approved Quality checklist is available before start of external plastering work

7.2. Cement, Fine Aggregates should be conforming to relevant standards. Ensure ratio of mortar mix and thickness of plaster is used as specified.

7.3. Work policies are to be monitored and are to be strictly implemented at site.

7.4. Ensure water proofing chemical is used in mortar mix as per manufacturer's recommendation for second coat or both coats as specified.

7.5. Ensure curing is done for minimum period of 7 days.

7.6. Check for line & plumb.

8. Safety:

8.1. Safety PPE's will be provided for workers.

8.2. First aid box will be provided at the site office.

8.3. Proper scaffolding should be done for external plastering work.

14

METHODOLOGY FOR WATERPROOFING WORKS- TOILET / UTILITY / SIT-OUT / BALCONY

1. Scope:

- This method provides a system of control for "Waterproofing Works- Toilet / Utility / Sit-Out / Balcony" in order to achieve compliance with the specifications and drawings.

2. Drawing Reference:

- Block Layout / Architectural Drawings / Relevant Drawings.

3. Equipment's:

➢ Trowel, Mixing Platform, Straight Edge, Measuring Box, Mixing Pan, Mixing tools for chemical, etc.

4. Tradesman:

➢ Water proofing contractor & workers.

5. Work Policy:

5.1. Waterproofing for Toilet/Utility/Sit-out /Balcony shall be started only after completion of minimum three floors of internal plastering in each block.

5.2. Waterproofing activity has to start from first floor onwards as the ground floor is mainly used for access and storage purpose. Ground floor waterproofing can be taken up at a later stage.

5.3. Before starting of waterproofing all the plumbing lines, electrical works in toilets should be completed including testing. Special care to be taken for connecting A.C drain pipe to floor trap.

5.4. Core cutting on floor to be marked by the plumbing engineer and precaution to be taken to do core cutting to the required sizes as specified viz. 125 mm for 110 mm dia, 90 mm for 75 mm dia etc.

5.5. Project Manager should allocate specific team for waterproofing works.

5.6. Proper lighting to be provided during the work, if required.

5.7. Removal of debris, rod cuttings if any, removal of laitance in the water proofing area has to be carried out prior to start of water proofing works and the execution team is responsible for this activity.

5.8. After removal of debris and cleaning of the area, Block In charge has to handover the floor to the waterproofing team.

5.9. Mockup should be done for every block and has to be approved.

6. Methodology:

6.1. In depth cleaning of the area and loose material removal with wire brush and using mechanical means is the responsibility of water proofing agency.

6.2. Manufactured and expiry dates of the material has to be checked prior to the commencement of water proofing works. Only sealed containers or packets are to be allowed.

6.3. Waterproofing for the entire floor toilets has to be started at a time.

6.4. PVC Sleeves should be fixed by the plumbing agency under the supervision of plumbing in charge.

6.5. Bore packing of the above floor has to be completed totally prior to the commencement of the water proofing of that particular floor.

6.6. Weep holes to be preferably located near the wet area floor trap, and the proposed protective plaster or screed must be sloped towards the weep hole.

6.7. Water proofing treatment has to be done as per the approved method statement of that particular applicator.

6.8. Check list format is to be pasted on the wall of the sunken area, so that one can know the actual status of work and the concerned person who has checked.

6.9. Access to be restricted to the water proofed area after completion of work.

6.10. Monthly reconciliation of waterproofing materials to be done to ascertain the actual consumption.

7. Quality Control & Quality Assurance:

7.1. Ensure approved Quality checklist is available before start of water proofing works at toilet, utility and sit out.

7.2. Water proofing materials should be conformed to the relevant standards.

7.3. Work policies are to be monitored and are to be strictly implemented at site.

7.4. Ensure Manufactured and expiry dates of the chemical.

7.5. Check for leakages and dampness on ceiling of lower floor.

8. Safety:

8.1. Safety PPE’s will be provided for workers.

8.2. First aid box will be provided at the site office.

15

METHODOLOGY FOR WATERPROOFING WORK -TERRACE

1. Scope:

- This method provides a system of control for "Waterproofing Work –Terrace" in order to attain compliance with the specifications and drawings.

2. Drawing Reference:

- Architectural Drawings / Relevant Drawings.

3. Equipment's:

- Trowel, Mixing Platform, Straight Edge, Measuring Box, Mixing Pan, Mixing tools for chemical, etc.

4. Tradesman:

- Water proofing contractor & workers.

5. Work Policy:

5.1. Before starting of waterproofing all the plumbing lines, electrical works should be completed including testing.

5.2. Plastering of head room, OHT, LMR, parapet and elevation elements must be completed prior to start of terrace waterproofing.

5.3. Removal of debris, rod cuttings if any, removal of laitance in the water proofing area has to be carried out prior to start of water proofing works and the execution team is responsible for this activity.

5.4. Mockup should be done for every block and has to be approved.

5.5. After removal of the debris and cleaning of the area, Block In charge has to handover the area to the water proofing team.

6. Methodology:

6.1. In depth cleaning of the area and loose material removal with wire brush and using mechanical means is the responsibility of water proofing agency.

6.2. For membrane coating, thickness of the membrane must be checked by cutting the 50 mm x 50 mm membrane sample at least one per flat.

6.3. Manufactured and expiry dates of the material has to be checked prior to the commencement of water proofing works. Only sealed containers or packs are to be allowed.

6.4. Water proofing treatment has to be done as per the approved method statement of that particular applicator.

6.5. Access to be restricted to the water proofed area after completion of work.

6.6. Monthly reconciliation of waterproofing materials is to be done to ascertain actual consumption.

7. Quality Control & Quality Assurance:

7.1. Ensure approved Quality checklist is available before start of water proofing work at terrace.

7.2. Water proofing materials should be conformed to relevant standards.

7.3. Work policies are to be monitored and are to be strictly implemented at site.

7.4. Ensure Manufactured and expiry dates of the material / chemical.

7.5. Check for leakages and dampness on ceiling of lower floor.

8. Safety:

8.1. Safety PPE's will be provided for workers.

8.2. First aid box will be provided at the site office.

16

METHODOLOGY FOR WATERPROOFING WORKS FOR PODIUM, RETAINING WALL, SWIMMING POOL, STP, UG SUMP, FIRE SUMP, GRADE SLAB & LIFT PITS

1. Scope:

- This method provides a system of control for "Waterproofing Work – Podium, Retaining Wall, Swimming Pool, STP, UG Sump, Fire Sump, Grade Slab and Lift Pits" in order to achieve compliance with the specifications and drawings.

2. Drawing Reference:

- Relevant Drawings.

3. Equipment's:

- Trowel, Mixing Platform, Straight Edge, Measuring Box, Mixing Pan, Mixing tools for chemical, etc.

4. Tradesman:

- Water proofing contractor & workers.

5. Work Policy:

5.1. Removal of debris, rod cuttings if any, removal of laitance in the water proofing area has to be carried out prior to start of water proofing works and the execution team is responsible for this activity.

5.2. After removal of the debris and cleaning of the area, Block In charge has to handover the area to the water proofing team.

5.3. Proper lighting to be provided during the work, if required.

6. Methodology:

6.1. In depth cleaning of the area and loose material removal with wire brush and using mechanical means is the responsibility of water proofing agency.

6.2. Defective concrete surface, construction joints & honeycomb area should be treated as per the manufacturer specification.

6.3. Junctions of raft and walls are to be treated as per the manufacturer specification.

6.4. Manufactured and expiry dates of the material has to be checked prior to the commencement of water proofing works. Only sealed containers or packs are to be allowed.

6.5. <u>Water proofing treatment has to be done as per the approved method statement of that particular applicator. Based on the approved methodology checklist to be prepared for all areas and approval must be obtained.</u>

6.6. Access to be restricted to the water proofed area after completion of work.

6.7. Monthly reconciliation of waterproofing material is to be done to ascertain the actual consumption.

7. Quality Control & Quality Assurance:

7.1. Ensure approved Quality checklist is available before start of water proofing for retaining walls, Sumps, Tanks, Grade slab.

7.2. Water proofing materials should be conforming to relevant standards.

7.3. Work policies are to be monitored and are to be strictly implemented at site.

7.4. Ensure Manufactured and expiry dates of the material / chemical.

7.5. Check for leakages and dampness by pond test.

8. Safety:

8.1. Safety PPE's will be provided for workers. First aid box will be provided at the site office.

17

METHODOLOGY FOR KITCHEN PLATFORMWORK

1. Scope:

➢ This method provides a system of control for "Kitchen Platform Work" in order to achieve compliance with the specifications and drawings.

2. Drawing Reference:

➢ Block Layout / Relevant Drawings.

3. Equipment's:

➢ Drilling machine, Cutting machine, Sprit level, Square ruler, Tube level, Measuring tape, etc.

4. Tradesman:

➢ Skilled Workers.

5. Work Policy:

5.1. Plastering and putty works must be completed prior to start of kitchen platform work

5.2. MEP clearance must be taken prior to start of kitchen platform work

5.3. All the dimensions of the MS angles must be checked as per the given specifications/drawings.

5.4. All MS members must be checked for bends, right angles, weld joints, grinding for weld joints etc.

5.5. Zinc chromate primer has to be applied to the angles.

5.6. Mockup has to be done for every block and has to be approved.

6. Methodology:

6.1. All members have to be fixed as per the given levels and specifications/drawings.

6.2. All angles have to be anchored properly and nut bolts must be properly tightened.

6.3. Granite used for platform shall be free from hair line cracks, flowers, moles, knots, white & dark lines etc.

6.4. Granite has to be checked for proper polishing and edge chamfering has to be done at the top and bottom.

6.5. Groove to be provided at the bottom of granite at a distance of 20 mm from the face for water drip.

6.6. Cutting for sink opening should not be more than 2 to 3 mm of sink size.

6.7. Gaps between angles and granite must be filled properly at regular intervals of 300 mm c/c with approved material.

6.8. Proper slope has to be provided for the granite at sink edges.

6.9. Proper protection must be done for the granite platform.

7. Quality Control & Quality Assurance:

7.1. Ensure approved Quality checklist is available before start of Kitchen platform work.

7.2. Work policies are to be monitored and are to be strictly implemented at site.

7.3. Check for line, level, right angle and dimensions.

8. Safety:

8.1. Safety PPE's will be provided for workers. First aid box will be provided at the site office.

18

METHODOLOGY FOR TILING WORK - DADO

1. Scope:

- This method provides a system of control for "Tiling Work – Dado" in order to achieve compliance with the specifications and drawings.

2. Drawing Reference:

- Block Layout / Architectural Drawings/ Relevant Drawings.

3. Equipment's:

- Tile cutting machine, Trowel, Mixing pan, wooden mallet, Plumb Bob, Sprit level, Square ruler, Tube level, line-dory, Measuring tape, etc.

4. Tradesman:

- Tile Layer / Masons & helpers.

5. Work Policy:

5.1. Tiling work shall be started only after completion of minimum three floors of waterproofing in each block.

5.2. Tiling work shall be started only after completion of external plastering of that block.

5.3. Before starting of tiling work, all the plumbing & electrical works should be completed including testing.

5.4. Floor level for the entire floor has to be established prior to the starting of tiling activity.

5.5. Location of ventilator has to be checked prior to start of the work.

5.6. Location of C.P & sanitary fittings, floor traps has to be ensured prior to starting of tiling work.

5.7. Concreting must be done in ledge walls at bracket location and is to be checked thoroughly prior to the commencement of tiling work.

5.8. Waterproofing has to be protected from damages and any physical damage should be intimated to waterproofing agency for doing the rectification of waterproofing treatment.

5.9. Sealant filing should be completed around ventilator before start of tiling work.

5.10. Cleanliness of the area has to be ensured by the execution team prior to the commencement of tiling works.

5.11. Material to be checked and segregated batch wise prior to the commencement of work.

5.12. Tiles to be soaked for 2 hrs prior to the usage.

5.13. Tiling Mockup along with cutting power tools has to be done for every block and has to be approved.

5.14. Proper lighting to be provided during the work, if required.

6. Methodology:

6.1. GFC drawings are to be pasted to the walls of the toilets by clearly mentioning the details like where to start, pattern of tiling etc.

6.2. Door location has to be checked w.r.t. E.W.C. position of that toilet.

6.3. Block In charge has to ensure the wall which is to be tiled is true to plumb and at right angles.

6.4. All concrete surfaces (For MIVAN Structure) hacking (50 to 60 nos. per SFT) should be done up to required level.

6.5. Plastering should be 12mm thickness and proportion of cement mortar should be CM 1:4.

6.6. Uniform cutting of tiles has to be done by mechanical means only at electrical and plumbing fixtures.

6.7. Back of the tile to be packed fully with cement paste before placing it in position.

6.8. After placement of tile, ensure to remove the entrapped air by tamping the tile with wooden mallet.

6.9. No tile pieces are allowed at the topmost layer.

6.10. Bottommost layer is to be laid only after completion of flooring.

6.11. Paper joints are to be provided for Dado portion.

6.12. Corner (door jamb / ventilator jamb / ledge wall) tiles edge should be cut at 45 degree (Miter Joint) and join at 90 degrees.

6.13. Curing has to be done for 3 days.

6.14. Hollowness test to be conducted, and if tiles with any hollowness (more than 5%) are found, they are to be replaced with new ones.

6.15. Grouting to be done before handing over of the flat.

6.16. Checklist format to be filled prior, during and the post completion of tiling work.

7. Quality Control & Quality Assurance:

7.1. Ensure approved Quality checklist is available before start of tiling.

7.2. Tiles should be conforming to relevant standards.

7.3. Ensure Tile brand, type & pattern has been used as approved.

7.4. Work policies are to be monitored and are to be strictly implemented at site.

7.5. Ensure Curing has been done for 3 days.

7.6. Check for Hollowness test on tiled surface.

7.7. Check for line, level, plumb, right angle, room dimensions& shade variation.

7.8. Ensure approved grouting material has been used and manufactured and expiry dates of the material.

8. Safety:

8.1. Safety PPE's will be provided for workers.

8.2. First aid box will be provided at the site office and good housekeeping will be ensured.

19

METHODOLOGY FOR TILING WORK - FLOORING

1. Scope:

- This method provides a system of control for "Tiling Work –Flooring" in order to achieve compliance with the specifications and drawings.

2. Drawing Reference:

- Block Layout / Architectural Drawings.

3. Equipment's:

- Tile cutting machine, Trowel, Mortar Mixing platform, Measuring box, Spade, Wooden mallet, Sprit level, Square ruler, Tube level, line-dory, Measuring tape, etc.

4. Tradesman:

- Tile Layers / Masons & helpers.

5. Work Policy:

5.1. Tiling work shall be started only after completion of minimum three floors of waterproofing in each block.

5.2. Tiling work shall be started only after completion of external plastering of that block.

5.3. Toilet/Utility dado must be completed prior to starting of flooring.

5.4. Tiling work shall be started only after completion of first coat of putty.

5.5. Before starting of tiling work, all the plumbing & electrical works should be completed including testing.

5.6. 1 m level (from FFL) marking should be done on all walls.

5.7. Floor level for the entire floor has to be established prior to the starting of tiling activity.

5.8. Location of C.P & sanitary fittings, floor traps has to be ensured prior to starting of tiling work.

5.9. Cleanliness of the area has to be ensured by the execution team prior to the commencement of tiling works.

5.10. Material to be checked and segregated batch wise prior to the commencement of work..

5.11. Ceramic tiles must be soaked for 2 hours prior to the usage.

5.12. Tiling Mockup has to be done for every block and has to be approved.

5.13. Proper lighting to be provided during the work, if required.

6. Methodology:

6.1. FFL of the flat must be 10 mm more than FFL of the Corridor.

6.2. Lift sill level must be 10 mm more than corridor flooring and gentle slope has to be given from lift sill to corridor floor.

6.3. GFC drawings are to be pasted to the walls by clearly mentioning the details like where to start, pattern of tiling, slopes etc.

6.4. Door location has to be checked w.r.t. E.W.C. position of that toilet.

6.5. Laying of mortar mix (CM 1:6 or as specified) at the base of the tiles.

6.6. Tiles must be laid first in the bed rooms and then in the living/dining area (tiles should be laid from the SLD to main door, no trespassing should be allowed).

6.7. 6mm gap to be maintained in tiling in all rooms/corridors along the walls to take care of thermal expansion/contraction.

6.8. Cement slurry @ 2 kg/ Sq. m to be laid on the mortar uniformly.

6.9. Raking on the mortar to be done so as to ensure proper bonding of the tile.

6.10. 6mm expansion joints must be provided in Drawing/ living room & corridors as per the drawing and PU sealant should be used for this joint.

6.11. While laying of tiles, proper tamping with wooden mallet has to be ensured to remove the entrapped air.

6.12. Uniform cutting of tiles has to be done by mechanical means only at floor traps.

6.13. During tiling care should be taken regarding the cutting of PVC pipes. Provide the protection caps or end caps to the UPVC pipes.

6.14. 2mm spacers are to be provided for ceramic flooring or refer architectural drawing.

6.15. 3mm spacers are to be provided for vitrified flooring or refer architectural drawing.

6.16. 8 mm Backer rod should be provided into the 6mm gap along the walls at all rooms/corridors to take care of thermal expansion/contraction.

6.17. Skirting tiles should be chamfered by 3 to 5mm or as specified.

6.18. Skirting should be laid at right angle to the floor and uniform top line should be maintained.

6.19. Skirting adjacent to the architrave must be laid only after fixing of architrave.

6.20. Curing has to be done for 3 days and checking for slopes has to be done.

6.21. Hollowness check to be done, and if tiles with any hollowness (more than 5%) or damages found, they are to be replaced with new ones or get them rectified.

6.22. Proper protection of tiles to be ensured after completion of work.

6.23. Grouting to be done before handing over of the flat.

6.24. Epoxy grouting has to be done for all areas except for toilet dado.

6.25. Checklist format to be filled prior, during and the post completion of tiling work.

7. Quality Control & Quality Assurance:

7.1. Ensure approved Quality checklist is available before start of Floor tiling.

7.2. Tiles should be conforming to relevant standards.

7.3. Ensure Tile brand, type & pattern has used as approved.

7.4. Work policies are to be monitored and are to be strictly implemented at site.

7.5. Ensure 6mm gap maintained in tiling in all rooms/corridors along the walls.

7.6. Ensure 6mm expansion joint provided in Drawing/ living room & corridors as per the drawing and PU sealant has been used.

7.7. Check for Hollowness test on tiled surface.

7.8. Check for line, level, right angle, room dimensions, evenness, shade variation, joint thickness & slope.

7.9. Ensure Curing has been done for 3 days.

7.10. Ensure approved epoxy grouting material& PU sealant has been used and manufactured& expiry dates of the material.

8. Safety:

8.1. Safety PPE's will be provided for workers.

8.2. First aid box will be provided at the site office and good housekeeping will be ensured.

20

METHODOLOGY FOR TILE DADO WORK – KITCHEN / WASH BASIN

1. Scope:

- ➢ This method provides a system of control for "Tiling Dado Work –Kitchen / Wash Basin" in order to attain compliance with the specifications and drawings.

2. Drawing Reference:

- Block Layout / Architectural Drawings / Relevant Drawings.

3. Equipment's:

- Tile cutting machine, Trowel, Mixing pan, wooden mallet, Plumb Bob, Sprit level, Square ruler, Tube level, line-dory, Measuring tape, etc.

4. Tradesman:

- Tile Layer / Masons & helpers.

5. Work Policy:

5.1. Tiling work shall be started only after completion of kitchen platform of minimum one floor.

5.2. Tiling work shall be started only after completion of fixing of kitchen window.

5.3. All plumbing & electrical works must be completed including testing prior to start of the dado work.

5.4. Fixing of utility door frame including architrave has to be completed prior to start of kitchen dado work.

5.5. Check must be done for roughened plaster surface prior to start of the work.

5.6. Tiles must be soaked for 2 hours prior to the usage.

5.7. Tiling Mockup has to be done for every block and has to be approved.

6. Methodology:

6.1. Dado work must be done as per the approved drawing.

6.2. Approved tile adhesive must be used for fixing of dado tile.

6.3. Grouting has to be done with approved material.

7. Quality Control & Quality Assurance:

7.1. Ensure approved Quality checklist is available before start of Kitchen and wash basin dado.

7.2. Tiles should be conforming to relevant standards.

7.3. Ensure Tile brand, type & pattern has been used as approved.

7.4. Work policies are to be monitored and are to be strictly implemented at site.

7.5. Ensure Curing has been done for 3 days.

7.6. Check for Hollowness test on tiled surface. Check for line, plumb& shade variation.

7.7. Ensure approved grouting / tile adhesive material has been used and manufactured & expiry dates of the material.

8. Safety:

8.1. Safety PPE's will be provided for workers. First aid box will be provided at the site office.

8.2. Proper illumination to be provided during the work, if required.

21

METHODOLOGY FOR FIXING OF UPVCWINDOWS /DOORS

1. Scope:

- This method provides a system of control for "Fixing of UPVC Windows/ Doors" in order to attain compliance with the specifications and drawings.

2. Drawing Reference:

- Joinery / Architectural Drawings.

3. Equipment's:

- Drilling machine, Sealant gun, Template, Sprit level, Measuring tape, etc.

4. Tradesman:

- UPVC Fixing Contractor & workers.

5. Work Policy:

5.1. For Windows:

5.1.1. Display board should be placed with all approved accessories, sealants etc.

5.1.2. Hardware of approved make should be used.

5.1.3. Internal Gypsum Plastering or at least wall bull marks must be completed prior to fixing of window frames for MIVAN structure.

5.1.4. Buffing & grinding of walls must be completed for MIVAN structure prior to fixing of window frames.

5.1.5. Sunshade top to be cleaned prior to frame installation.

5.1.6. Template checking and aperture rectifications must be completed prior to fixing of windows.

5.1.7. Window frames must be checked for dimensions, any defects, cracks, twists etc.

5.1.8.5 mm to 7 mm gap must be ensured all-round the frame for sealant provision.

5.1.9. Sealant must be completed prior to application of Chajja bottom skim coat.

5.1.10. Tiling works must be completed prior to fixing of window shutters and glass.

5.1.11. 2nd coat putty works must be completed prior to fixing windows shutters and glass.

5.1.12. External texture must be completed prior to fixing of window shutters and glass.

5.1.13. Window glass must be checked for thickness, colour, toughened, scratches.

5.1.14. Mockup has to be done for every block and has to be approved.

5.2. For Doors:

5.2.1. Display board should be placed with all approved accessories, sealants etc.

5.2.2. Hardware of approved make should be used.

5.2.3. Buffing & grinding of walls must be completed for MIVAN structure prior to fixing of door frames.

5.2.4. Template checking and aperture rectifications must be completed prior to fixing of door.

5.2.5. Door frames must be checked for dimensions, any defects, cracks, twists etc.

5.2.6.5 mm gap must be ensured all-round the frame for sealant provision.

5.2.7. Tiling works must be completed prior to fixing of door frame.

5.2.8. 2nd coat putty works must be completed prior to fixing of door frame.

5.2.9. Door glass must be checked for thickness, colour, toughened, scratches.

5.2.10. Mockup has to be done for every block and has to be approved.

6. Methodology:

6.1. Alignment of window / door frame must be checked while fixing.

6.2. Only SS hardware to be used for window / door.

6.3. Proper cleaning must be ensured prior to sealant filling.

6.4. Acrylic sealant for internal and silicone sealant for external face must be used.

6.5. All accessories like keeps, shutter stoppers, drain caps, screw caps, wool piles, anti-lift blocks, hinges, etc. are to be properly fixed.

6.6. Touch locks must be in good working condition and free movement of shutters and rigidity are to be ensured.

6.7. Leakage test for window / door must be done by splashing of water from the external side.

6.8. Protection tape from the window / door should not be removed till the completion of painting works.

7. Quality Control & Quality Assurance:

7.1. Ensure approved Quality checklist is available before start of UPVC Windows and doors.

7.2. Work policies are to be monitored and are to be strictly implemented in site.

7.3. Check for verticality, alignment of window / door frame, type, dimensions, fixing of all accessories, free movement of shutters and rigidity.

7.4. Ensure equal distance of ventilator / window jamb from inside.

7.5. Ensure only SS hardware is used as approved and protection tape from ventilator /window / door should not be removed till the completion of painting works.

7.6. Ensure masking tape has been provided before filling of sealant and has been removed after filling of sealant. Ensure acrylic sealant for internal & silicone sealant for external face was used as approved.

7.7. Ensure good housekeeping and see that the empty sealants cans are to be properly disposed

7.8. Check for leakage test for windows.

8. Safety:

8.1. Safety PPE's will be provided for workers and First aid box will be provided at the site office.

8.2. Proper illumination to be provided during the work, if required.

22

METHODOLOGY FOR FIXING OF ALUMINIUM VENTILATORS

1. Scope:

- This method provides a system of control for "Fixing of Aluminium Ventilators" in order to attain compliance with the specifications and drawings.

2. Drawing Reference:

- Furniture / Architectural Drawings / Relevant Drawings.

3. Equipment's:

- Drilling machine, Sealant gun, Template, Sprit level, Measuring tape, etc.

4. Tradesman:

- Aluminium Ventilator Fixing Contractor& workers.

5. Work Policy:

5.1. External plastering must be completed prior to fixing of ventilators.

5.2. Template checking and aperture rectifications if any must be completed prior to fixing of ventilators.

5.3. 5 mm to 7 mm gap must be ensured all-round the frame for sealant provision.

5.4. Ventilator must be checked for dimensions, any defects, cracks, twists etc.

5.5. Ventilator glass must be checked for thickness, colour, toughened.

5.6. Mockup has to be done for every block and has to be approved.

6. Methodology:

6.1. Alignment of ventilator must be checked while fixing.

6.2. Only SS hardware to be used for ventilator.

6.3. Proper cleaning must be ensured prior to sealant filling.

6.4. Acrylic sealant for internal and silicone sealant for external face must be used.

6.5. All accessories like keeps, shutter stoppers, drain caps, screw caps, wool piles etc. are to be properly fixed.

6.6. Touch locks must be in good working condition and free movement of shutters and rigidity are to be ensured.

6.7. Leakage test for ventilators must be done by splashing of water from the external side.

7.Quality Control & Quality Assurance:

7.1. Ensure approved Quality checklist is available before start of ventilator fixing

7.2. Work policies are to be monitored and are to be strictly implemented in site.

7.3. Check for verticality, alignment of ventilator frame, dimensions, all accessories are fixed, free movement of shutters and rigidity.

7.4. Ensure equal distance of ventilator frame from inner face.

7.5. Ensure only SS hardware has been used as approved.

7.6. Ensure masking tape has been provided before filling of sealant and has been removed after filling of sealant. Ensure acrylic sealant for internal & silicone sealant for external face has used as approved.

7.7. Check for leakage test for ventilator.

8. Safety:

8.1. Safety PPE's will be provided for workers and First aid box will be provided at the site office.

8.2. Proper illumination to be provided during the work, if required.

23

METHODOLOGY FOR FIXING OF DOOR FRAMES

1. Scope:

- This method provides a system of control for "Fixing of Door Frames" in order to attain compliance with the specifications and drawings.

2. Drawing Reference:

- Joinery / Architectural Drawings / Relevant Drawing.

3. Equipment's:

- Hammer, Sprit level, Square ruler, Measuring tape, etc.

4. Tradesman:

- Carpenter & helpers.

5. Work Policy:

5.1. All door frames in a particular floor in all flats have to be fixed simultaneously.

5.2. All door frames have to be checked prior to fixing for any bends, cracks.

5.3. Levels have to be cross checked prior to fixing of door frames. Previous levels marked as reference for doing plumbing works/ lintel works etc. are to be taken as the reference for fixing of door frames. Any deviation noticed in heights shall be intimated to the project heads/MEP heads.

5.4. Mockup has to be done for every block and has to be approved.

6. Methodology:

6.1. All the door frames have to be fixed as per the given levels.

6.2. 15 mm gap has to be maintained all round the frame for PU foam sealant.

6.3. Check for verticality, alignment of door frame, type &dimensions as per specification.

6.4. Mist the surface prior to foam application.

6.5. Gaps have to be filled with PU foam.

6.6. Excess foam has to be cut and air cured for 2 days.

6.7. Cover the PU foam with painting putty neatly after air curing for 2 days.

6.8. For main and utility door frames, in addition to PU foam, frame has to be fixed to the walls with three anchor fasteners on each side of the frame.

7. Quality Control & Quality Assurance:

7.1. Ensure approved Quality checklist is available before start of door frame fixing

7.2. Ensure type of door frame used as approved.

7.3. Work policies are to be monitored and are to be strictly implemented at site.

7.4. Ensure for verticality, alignment of door frame, dimensions& moisture content as per specification.

7.5. Ensure 15mm gap filled all sides of the frame with approved PU foam.

8. Safety:

8.1. Safety PPE's will be provided for workers and First aid box will be provided at the site office.

24

METHODOLOGY FOR FIXING OF DOOR SHUTTERS

1. Scope:

- This method provides a system of control for "Fixing of Door Shutters" in order to attain compliance with the specifications and drawings.

2. Drawing Reference:

- Joinery / Architectural Drawings / Relevant Drawings.

3. Equipment's:

- Sprit level, Square ruler, Measuring tape, etc.

4. Tradesman:

- Carpenter & helpers.

5. Work Policy:

5.1. Tiling work must be completed prior to fixing of door shutters.

5.2. Primer must be applied to the door shutter and architraves prior to fixing.

5.3. All door shutters in a particular floor in all flats have to be fixed simultaneously.

5.4. All door shutters have to be checked prior to fixing for any defects (bends, cracks, damages, etc).

5.5. Mockup has to be done for every block and has to be approved.

6. Methodology:

6.1. All hinges, screws to be fixed properly (3 hinges for internal and 4 hinges for main door shutters).

6.2. <u>3mm gap for top, sides & 5 mm gap for bottom to be maintained between door frame and shutter after finishing.</u>

6.3. Check for dimensions, verticality and alignment of door shutter as per specification.

6.4. Door hardware should be fixed as per the specifications.

6.5. Cylindrical locks should not be provided for Utilities / Balconies.

6.6. 2 mm gap must be provided for the architraves at the bottom.

6.7. All the hardware should be properly protected.

7. Quality Control & Quality Assurance:

7.1. Ensure approved Quality checklist is available before start of door shutter fixing

7.2. Material should be conforming to relevant standards.

7.3. Ensure make, dimensions as pre the drawing/specification, if any defects (bends, cracks, damages, etc) of door shutter & hardware to be checked before fixing.

7.4. Work policies are to be monitored and are to be strictly implemented at site.

7.5. Ensure for verticality & alignment of door shutter.

7.6. Ensure 3mm gap for top & sides and 5 mm gap for bottom provided between door frame and shutter after finishing, smooth operations.

7.7. Ensure all hinges, screws are properly (3 hinges for internal and 4 hinges for main door shutters) fixed.

7.8. Ensure 2 mm gap provided for the architraves at the bottom.

8. Safety:

8.1. Safety PPE's will be provided for workers. First aid box will be provided at the site office.

25

METHODOLOGY FOR TANDUR FLOORING – STAIRCASE

1. Scope:

- This method provides a system of control for "Tandur Flooring– Staircase" in order to attain compliance with the specifications and drawings.

2. Drawing Reference:

- Architectural Drawings / Relevant Drawings.

3. Equipment's:

- Cutting machine, Trowel, Mortar Mixing platform, Measuring box, Spade, Wooden mallet, Sprit level, Square Ruler, Tube level, line-dory, Measuring tape, etc.

4. Tradesman:

- Masons & helpers.

5. Work Policy:

5.1. Staircase plastering must be completed prior to start of Tandur works.

5.2. Ensure that the wall plastering is not done for skirting portion up to 200 mm from the floor.

5.3. Ensure proper surface preparation for the staircase including dead mortar chipping, cleaning etc. prior to the starting of work.

5.4. Floor level should be marked at mid landing and landing area.

5.5. Levels should be checked thoroughly between floor to mid landing and vice versa and ensure that the stair case FFL must match with the corridor FFL.

5.6. Material used for flooring should be sound, durable with specified dimensions and free from defects like cracks, knots, cavities etc.

5.7. Tread length and riser heights must be as per the approved sizes and edges must be chamfered prior to laying as per the requirement.

5.8. Mockup has to be done for every block and has to be approved.

5.9. Proper lighting to be provided during the work, if required.

6. Methodology:

6.1. Tread must be seated over the riser completely without any gaps with proper alignment.

6.2. 3 to 5 mm nosing must be provided.

6.3. Riser must be seated over the tread completely and it should be laid with proper vertical alignment.

6.4. Ensure specified mix proportion of mortar and it should be spread over the base area as per the specified thickness.

6.5. Slabs are to be fixed over the mortar bed with cement slurry, to be pressed and tamped with wooden mallet to bring it to the true level surface.

6.6. Proper check must be done for edge finish, pattern, slope (at landing), level, right angle

& dimensions.

6.7. Skirting should be laid at right angle to the tread and riser.

6.8. Treads and skirting's should be chamfered by 3 to 5mm properly.

6.9. Groove of 12 mm width x 6 mm depth is to be maintained alongside the tread and riser in the plastering.

6.10. Curing should be done for 3 days.

6.11. Check must be done for 5 coats polishing of the surface.

6.12. Check must be done for proper cleaning and protection of the surface.

7. Quality Control & Quality Assurance:

7.1. Ensure approved Quality checklist is available before start of Tandoor flooring for stair case.

7.2. Cement, Fine Aggregates & Tandur Stone should be conforming to relevant standards.

Ensure ratio of mortar mix and thickness of plaster is used as specified.

7.3. Work policies are to be monitored and are to be strictly implemented at site.

7.4. Ensure 3 to 5 mm nosing has been provided.

7.5. Ensure for edge finish, pattern, slope, level, right angle, groove & dimensions.

7.6. Ensure 5 coats polished on the surface and protection of the surface.

7.7. Ensure Curing has been done for 3 days.

8.Safety:

8.1. Safety PPE's will be provided for workers.

8.2. First aid box will be provided at the site office and good housekeeping will be ensured.

26

METHODOLOGY FOR INTERNAL PAINTING WORKS

1. Scope:

- This method provides a system of control for "Internal Painting Works - Internal Walls, Ceilings and Internal Doors" in order to attain compliance with the specifications and drawings.

2. Drawing Reference:

- Architectural Drawings / Relevant Drawings.

3. Equipment's:

- Finishing Trowel, Aluminium Straight Edge, Sand paper, Roller / Brush, etc.

4. Tradesman:

- Punning Masons, Painters & helpers.

5. Work Policy:

5.1. Internal plastering including sit-out, utility, ODU's, door frame fixing, UPVC window frames fixing& railing check lists must be closed prior to putty application.

5.2. External plastering for particular area should be completed.

5.3. All the snag points should be attended before putty application.

5.4. Cracks are to be properly treated prior to application of putty.

5.5. MEP clearance is to be taken before putty application.

5.6. DB & Electrical box alignments to be ensured in addition to MEP clearance.

5.7. Surface preparation should be done by stoning prior to putty application.

5.8. Tile skirting top, electrical switch boards & door hardware must be protected.

5.9. UPVC windows shutter fixing, tiling, door shutter check lists must be closed prior to primer application.

5.10. All MEP testing, tile grouting, CP & sanitary fittings should be completed before second coat of paint.

5.11. Proper lighting to be provided during the work, if required.

5.12. Mockup has to be done for every block and has to be approved.

6. Methodology:

6.1. Clean the surface from dirt, dust, grease, loose particles etc. and superfine putty has to be applied for interior walls, ceiling and skim coat for utility, sit out, corridor and staircase areas.

6.2. POP punning to be done in between tile dado and false ceiling in toilets and a groove of 8 mm x 4 mm to be provided in the punning above dado.

6.3. Surface must be kept ready for primer by sand papering and proper cleaning with cloth.

6.4. Light checking must be done for surface undulations and are to be rectified before primer application.

6.5. Application of primer & emulsion paint on walls & ceilings should be done by using roller and corners should be finished by using brush.

6.6. Application of primer must be done as per the manufacturer specification.

6.7. All touch up works and surface undulations if any observed in light checking(after primer) are to be rectified for perfect line and level by using POP or putty wherever required before 1st coat paint.

6.8. All the door frames and door shutter sides should be primed, KPF putty to be applied and also base coat preparation should be done for main door polish.

6.9. Doors painting must be completed as per specification.

6.10. Apply 1st coat of emulsion paint for walls as per the manufacturer specification.

6.11. Apply 2 coats of emulsion paint as per manufacturer specification.

6.12. Apply second coat of emulsion paint as per the manufacturer specification.

6.13. Polish should be applied to main door.

7. Quality Control & Quality Assurance:

7.1. Ensure approved Quality checklist is available before start of internal painting.

7.2. Ensure POP, putty& primer has been used as approved.

7.3. Ensure paint brand, type & colour has been used as specified / approved.

7.4. Work policies are to be monitored and are to be strictly implemented at site.

7.5. Ensure light checking has been done for surface undulations.

7.6. Ensure uniform application of primer & paint on the internal walls & ceilings and internal doors as per manufacturer specification.

8.Safety:

8.1. Safety PPE's will be provided for workers.

8.2. First aid box will be provided at the site office and good housekeeping will be ensured.

8.3. Proper platform to be made for wall height and ceiling.

27

METHODOLOGY FOR EXTERNAL PAINTING WORK

1. Scope:

- This method provides a system of control for "External Painting Work – Walls" in order to attain compliance with the specifications and drawings.

2. Drawing Reference:

- Elevation / Architectural Drawings.

3. Equipment's:

- Finishing Trowel, Roller / Brush, etc.

4. Tradesman:

- Painters & helpers.

5. Work Policy:

5.1. External plastering, UPVC window frames fixing including sealant application and waterproofing works must be completed prior to texture application.

5.2. All the snag points should be attended before texture application.

5.3. Proper scaffolding should be erected for external painting work.

5.4. Cracks are to be properly treated prior to application of texture.

5.5. Moisture content of walls should not exceed 12% prior to texture application.

5.6. Ensure proper cleaning of chajjas & band patties prior to texture/paint application.

5.7. Mockup has to be done at site for every block and approval to be taken from the client prior to commencement of main work.

6. Methodology:

6.1. Surface preparation should be done by stoning & surface shall be free from dirt, dust, grease, loose particles etc. prior to texture application.

6.2. Approved texture pattern must be applied as per the drawing and manufacturer specification.

6.3. Abro tape must be provided at break up joints.

6.4. First coat paint must be applied as per the manufacturer specification and architectural drawings.

6.5. Coarse threaded external rollers as approved by the manufacturer must be used for the paint application.

6.6. Abro tape must be used at the junctions of the different shades of paint.

6.7. Second coat paint must be applied as per the manufacturer specification and architectural drawings.

7. Quality Control & Quality Assurance:

7.1. Ensure approved Quality checklist is available before start of external painting.

7.2. Ensure texture & paint brand, type / pattern & colour has been used as approved.

7.3. Work policies are to be monitored and are to be strictly implemented at site.

7.4. Ensure uniform application of texture, primer & paint on the external walls as per manufacturer specification.

7.5. Ensure Abro tape has been provided at the junctions of the different shades of paint.

8. Safety:

8.1. Safety PPE's will be provided for workers.

8.2. First aid box will be provided at the site office.

28

METHODOLOGY FOR VACUUM DEWATERED FLOORING

1. Scope:

➢ This method provides a system of control for "Vacuum Dewatered Flooring" in order to attain compliance with the specifications and drawings.

2. Drawing Reference:

➢ Floor Plan, Structural& Relevant Drawing.

3. Equipment's:

➢ Auto Level with accessories, Steel cutting & bending machine, RMC Plant / Concrete Mixer, Transit Mixer, MS side track rails, Screed Vibrator, Vacuum Dewatering machine with accessories, Mechanical Floater, etc.

4. Tradesman:

- Operators, Drivers, Bar bender, Masons & helpers.

5.Work Policy:

5.1. Surface should be cleaned thoroughly prior to the screed pour.

5.2. MS side track rails must be placed as per the required level and to the required gradient.

5.3. Leveling beam and surface vibrator must be erected over the side track rails.

5.4. Stop ends should be provided with MS arrangement.

5.5. Proper illumination will be provided, if required.

6. Methodology:

6.1. For podiums use only approved M 25 grade fiber reinforced screed concrete/or as mentioned in BOQ.

6.2. For cellars use approved M 15/M 20 grade screed concrete.

6.3. Approved polythene sheet must be placed prior to placement of grade slab reinforcement

6.4. Water proofing admixture should be added in the concrete mix as specified.

6.5. 40 mm needle vibrator should be used for vibration of concrete.

6.6. After completion of 5 to 6 Sq.m, the surface vibrator shall be run over the concrete surface.

6.7. Surface vibrator should be run along with leveling beam for the second time over the finished concrete surface.

6.8. Vacuum mat must be placed over the levelled concrete surface to suck off excess water at the rate of 2 minutes per centimeter thickness of slab.

6.9. Floating operation should be started after removal of mat with power operated skin floater till desired finish is obtained.

6.10. Alternate panels should be casted to minimize cracking at the construction joints.

6.11. Broom finish should be done for podium screed and smooth finish for cellars.

6.12. Check for VDF top levels & slope.

6.13. Curing by ponding must be done for a minimum period of 7 days.

6.14. Vehicle movement should not be allowed till 28 days of placement of screed.

6.15. Groove cutting must be done within 7 days of placement of screed.

6.16. Width of the groove should be 5 mm.

6.17. Depth of groove should be 1/4th to 1/3rd of the slab thickness and should not be less than 25 mm.

6.18. Spacing of the grooves must be 24 to 36 times thickness of the slab and should not be more than 4.50 m.

6.19. Grooved panel size should not exceed 12 Sq.m.

6.20. Panels between joints should be square/rectangle and the length should not exceed 1.5 times the width.

6.21. Grooves must be filled with sealant after 28 days of placement of screed

7. Quality Control & Quality Assurance:

7.1. Ensure approved Quality checklist is available before start of VDF Flooring.

7.2. Cement, Fine Aggregates, Coarse Aggregates, Water, Fly ash / GGBFS, Chemical Admixtures& Water proofing admixture should be conforming to relevant standards. Ensure approved mix design& proper grade of concrete has been used.

7.3. Ensure water proofing admixture has been added in concrete mix as specified.

7.4. Work policies are to be monitored and are to be strictly implemented at site.

7.5. Sampling of concrete cubes for 7 days & 28 days compressive strength, ensure the compressive strength for 7 days & 28 days achieved as specified. Slump test to be conducted at site.

7.6. Ensure Vacuum dewatering system has been done properly.

7.7. Ensure broom finish has been done for podium screed and smooth finish for cellars.

7.8. Ensure for VDF top levels of concrete & slope.

7.9. Ensure panel size, groove cutting and groove filling with approved sealant as specified.

7.10. Ensure curing has been done for minimum 7 days.

7.11. Ensure vehicular movement has not been allowed till 28 days of placement of screed.

8. Safety:

1.1. Safety PPE's will be provided for workers.

1.2. First aid box will be provided at the site office.

29

METHODOLOGY FOR SCREED WORK

1. Scope:

➢ This method provides a system of control for "Screed Work" in order to attain compliance with the specifications and drawings.

2. Drawing Reference:

➢ Floor Plan / Relevant Drawings.

3. Equipment's:

➢ Auto Level with accessories, RMC Plant / Concrete Mixer, Transit Mixer, Vibrator, Finishing tools, etc.

4. Tradesman:

➢ Operators, Drivers, Masons & helpers.

5. Work Policy:

5.1. Surface should be cleaned thoroughly prior to the screed pour.

5.2. Level pads must be placed as per the required level and to the required gradient.

5.3. Proper lighting should be provided, if required.

5.4. For terrace use only approved M 20 grade(/or as specified in the drawings & spec) fiber reinforced & waterproofing screed concrete.

5.5. For rooms in the flats, hardscaping areas etc. use approved grade of screed concrete.

6. Methodology:

6.1. Proper vibration should be done

6.2. Broom finish should be done for screed concrete.

6.3. Screed top levels & slope should be checked

6.4. Curing by ponding must be done for a minimum period of 7 days.

6.5. Groove cutting must be done within 7 days of placement of screed for terrace

6.6. Width of the groove should be 5 mm.

6.7. Depth of groove should be 1/4th to 1/3rd of the slab thickness and should not be less than 15 mm.

6.8. Spacing of the grooves must be 24 to 36 times thickness of the slab and should not be more than 4.50 m.

6.9. Panel size should not exceed 10sq.m.

6.10. Panels between joints should be square/rectangle and the length should not exceed 1.5 times the width.

6.11. Grooves must be filled with sealant after completion of curing period

7. Quality Control & Quality Assurance:

7.1. Ensure approved Quality checklist is available before start of screed.

7.2. Cement, Fine Aggregates, Coarse Aggregates, Water, Fly ash / GGBFS, Chemical Admixtures& Water proofing admixture should be conforming to relevant standards. Ensure approved mix design& proper grade of concrete has been used.

7.3. Ensure water proofing admixture/fibers have been added in concrete mix as specified.

7.4. Work policies are to be monitored and are to be strictly implemented at site.

7.5. Sampling and testing of concrete for workability &compressive strength should be done

7.6. Ensure broom finish for the finished surface

7.7. Check for top levels of screed.

7.8. Ensure panel size, groove cutting and groove filling with approved sealant as specified.

7.9. Ensure curing has been done for minimum 7days.

8. Safety:

8.1. Safety PPE's will be provided for workers.

8.2. First aid box will be provided at the site office.

8.3. Proper lighting should be provided, if required.

30

METHODOLOGY FOR RUBBLE SOLING WORK

1. Scope:

- This method provides a system of control for "Rubble Soling Work" in order to attain compliance with the specifications and drawings.

2. Drawing Reference:

- Relevant Drawing.

3. Equipment's:

- Dumpers, Static Roller – 3 MT, etc.

4. Tradesman:

- Operators, Drivers, Masons & Helpers.

5. Work Policy:

5.1. The stone should be hard, durable and free from defects. The rubble should be of suitable size and shape to give the required compacted thickness.

6. Methodology:

6.1. The rubble is laid in vertical position of the sub-grade but closely packed by arranging the stones.

6.2. The filling of the gaps shall be done with quarry stones as required simultaneously with the placing of the rubble.

6.3. Ramming near the walls and column shall be done properly to the required level / slope, camber etc.

6.4. Compaction must be carried out with 3 MT static roller as required.

6.5. The finishing of the surface shall be done by trimming to required level / slope as per requirement.

7. Quality Control & Quality Assurance:

7.1. Ensure approved Quality checklist is available before start of rubble soling.

7.2. Material should be conforming to relevant standards.

7.3. Work policy to be monitored and are to be strictly implemented at site.

7.4. Ensure compaction has been done as required.

8. Safety:

8.1. Safety PPE's will be provided for workers.

8.2. First aid box will be provided at the site office.

31

METHODOLOGY FOR STONE MASONRY WORK

1. Scope:

- This method provides a system of control for "Stone Masonry Work" in order to attain compliance with the specifications and drawings.

2. Drawing Reference:

- Architectural / Relevant Drawings.

3. Equipment's:

- Trowel, Spade, Measuring Box, Water Drum, Plumb Bob, Straight edge, Tube level, line- dory, Measuring tape, etc.

4. Tradesman:

- Masons & helpers.

5. Work Policy:

5.1. Stone to be used in masonry should be granite, quartzite, gneiss, laterite or any other type of good stone as specified.

5.2. All stones should be free from defects like cracks, cavities, sand holes, flaws etc. and the water absorption shall not exceed 5%.

5.3. The size of stone shall not be less than 150 mm in any direction. The height of the stone may be up to 300 mm. Round faced stones should not be used.

5.4. Dressing and shaping of stone shall be done prior to be used in masonry

6. Methodology:

6.1. Mortar proportion should be as specified and thickness of joints shall be up to 20 mm.

6.2. The height of wall construction should not exceed one meter per day.

6.3. Corner stones are to be dressed up to 50 mm wide on both sides perfectly at right angles.

6.4. Key/Bond stones are to be provided at an interval of not exceeding 2 m.

6.5. Stone should overlap by at least 300 mm at their tails wherever possible.

6.6. No voids are to be left inside the masonry works.

6.7. Provide DPC, expansion joints & weep holes as per the drawing.

6.8. Curing of masonry works shall be carried out for minimum 7 days.

7. Quality Control & Quality Assurance:

7.1. Ensure approved Quality checklist is available before start of stone masonry.

7.2. Stone, Cement, Fine Aggregates should be conforming to relevant standards. Ensure ratio of mortar mix and thickness of mortar has been used as specified.

7.3. Work policies are to be monitored and are to be strictly implemented at site.

7.4. Ensure DPC, expansion joints & weep holes are provided as per the drawing.

7.5. Ensure curing of masonry works has been carried out for minimum 7 days.

8. Safety:

8.1. Safety PPE's will be provided for workers. First aid box will be provided at the site office.

32

METHODOLOGY FOR EXPANSION JOINT TREATMENT

1. Scope:

- This method provides a system of control for "Expansion Joint Treatment for Vertical and Horizontal Surfaces" in order to attain compliance with the specifications and drawings.

2. Drawing Reference:

- Floor Plan / Relevant Drawings.

3. Equipment's:

- Wire brush, Sealant gun, etc.

4. Tradesman:

- Mason & helpers.

5. Work Policy:

5.1. The joints of the proposed expansion joint must be cleaned thoroughly using wire brush, blowers etc. to remove fine debris.

5.2. Damaged edges of the expansion joint must be treated with Epoxy resin mortar.

5.3. Mockup has to be done and has to be approved.

6. Methodology:

6.1. Existing joint filler board must be removed for a depth of 50mm.

6.2. Backer rod must be inserted and primer should be applied to the expansion joint side surfaces.

6.3. When primary is in sticky condition, approved sealant has to be applied as per the manufacturer specification. (Generally depth of sealant is half of width of joint).

6.4. The Sealant has to be applied with Sealant gun in a continuous bead to fill the joint completely.

6.5. Sealant has to be filled in the joint as per the Standard norms and procedures given by the manufacturer.

6.6. Allow the joint for air cure as specified by the manufacturer.

6.7. Check for any leakages by pond test for 24 hours.

6.8. Proper protection of the expansion joint has to be ensured.

6.9. Heavy duty joint filler board 'Dura board HD 100' has to be used in the screed concrete over the expansion joint portion.

7. Quality Control & Quality Assurance:

7.1. Ensure approved Quality checklist is available before start of expansion joint treatment

7.2. Expansion joint materials should be conformed to relevant standards.

7.3. Work policies are to be monitored and are to be strictly implemented at site.

7.4. Ensure approved sealant has been applied as per the manufacturer specification.

7.5. Ensure proper protection of the expansion joint.

8. Safety:

8.1. Safety PPE's will be provided for workers and First aid box will be provided at the site office.

33

METHODOLOGY FOR FIXING OF MS DOOR / ALUMINIUM LOUVER FOR SHAFTS

1. Scope:

- This method provides a system of control for "Fixing of MS Door / Aluminium Louver for Shafts" in order to attain compliance with the specifications and drawings.

2. Drawing Reference:

- Architectural/ Relevant Drawings.

3. Equipment's:

- Drilling machine, Template, Sprit level, Measuring tape, etc.

4. Tradesman:

- Door fixing contractor & workers.

5. Work Policy:

5.1. Plastering and flooring works must be completed prior to fixing of shaft doors.

5.2. Template checking and aperture rectifications must be completed prior to fixing of doors.

5.3. 3 to 4 mm gap must be ensured all-round the door frame prior to fixing.

5.4. Door frames must be checked for dimensions, any defects, bends etc.

5.5. Mockup has to be done for every block and has to be approved.

6. Methodology:

6.1. Frames are to be fixed properly with anchor bolts and alignment of door frame must be checked while fixing.

6.2. Alignment of door shutter also to be checked during fixing.

6.3. Hardware to be fixed to the doors as per the requirement.

7. Quality Control & Quality Assurance:

7.1. Ensure approved Quality checklist is available before start of fixing MS doors & aluminum louvers for shafts.

7.2. Work policies are to be monitored and are to be strictly implemented at site.

7.3. Check for verticality, alignment & dimensions of door frame and shutter.

7.4. Ensure hardware's are fixed to the door as per the requirement.

8. Safety:

8.1. Safety PPE's will be provided for workers.

8.2. First aid box will be provided at the site office.

34

METHODOLOGY FOR TOILET FALSE CEILING WORK

1. Scope:

➢ This method provides a system of control for “Toilet False Ceiling Work” in order to attain compliance with the specifications and drawings.

2. Drawing Reference:

➢ Furniture / Architectural/ Ceiling Lay out Drawings.

3. Equipment’s:

➢ Drilling machine, Sprit level, Tube level, Measuring tape, etc.

4. Tradesman:

➢ False ceiling fixing contractor & workers.

5. Work Policy:

5.1. Ensure that plastering works must be completed up to the required height.

5.2. Ensure that POP punning works shall be done above the toilet dado up to the required height.

5.3. MEP works must be completed and clearance to be taken from concerned MEP Engineer prior to start of the work.

5.4. Ensure that approved materials are available at site as per the shop drawings.

5.5. Mockup has to be done for every block and has to be approved.

6. Methodology:

6.1. Angles shall be fixed with screws and plugs as per the approved section details of false ceiling.

6.2. Grids shall be laid out as per the approved ceiling layout.

6.3. Hangers must be installed as per the spacing and level required.

6.4. Main T sections shall be fixed to the hangers as per approved drawing.

6.5. Cross T bars shall be fixed in between main T sections to its lock positions perpendicular to it.

6.6. Leveling shall be carried out to prevent any subsequent downward movement.

6.7. During the installation process care must be taken to prevent damages to MEP works and waterproofing system.

6.8. Ceiling boards are to be fixed after ensuring final adjustment of framing and entire suspension level.

7. Quality Control & Quality Assurance:

7.1. Ensure approved Quality checklist is available before start false celling for toilet

7.2. False ceiling boards and frames should be conforming to the relevant standards.

7.3. Ensure false ceiling board make, type & thickness has been used as approved.

7.4. Work policies are to be monitored and are to be strictly implemented at site.

7.5. Ensure grids are laid out as per the approved ceiling layout.

7.6. Check for alignment& level of bottom of ceiling, dimensions of frame work and false ceiling board joint evenness.

8. Safety:

8.1. Safety PPE's will be provided for workers and First aid box will be provided at the site office.

35

METHODOLOGY FOR GRANITE / MARBLE WORK - LIFT LOBBY - FLOORING

1. Scope:

- This method provides a system of control for "Granite / Marble work – Lift Lobby Flooring" in order to attain compliance with the specifications and drawings.

2. Drawing Reference:

- Architectural Drawings / Relevant Drawings.

3. Equipment's:

- Granite / Marble cutting machine, Trowel, Mortar Mixing platform, Measuring box, Spade, Wooden mallet, Sprit level, Square ruler, Tube level, line-dory, Measuring tape, Polishing Machine etc.

4. Tradesman:

- Granite / Marble Layers / Masons & helpers.

5. Work Policy:

5.1. Flooring work shall be started only after completion of Entire Tower Block work, Plastering in Lift lobby.

5.2. Flooring work shall be started only after Lift Frame erection of all floors including basements.

5.3. Before starting of flooring work, all the MEP works should be completed including testing.

5.4. 1 m level (from FFL) marking should be done on lobby walls.

5.5. Floor level has to be established and cross checked with Lift frame fixed.

5.6. Cleanliness of the area has to be ensured by the execution team prior to the commencement of flooring works.

5.7. Material to be checked and segregated for Approved uniform color, texture, thickness and for defects if any.

5.8. Every granite stones/ granite tile should be cut to the required size and pre polished as per drawing.

5.9. Flooring Mockup has to be done for every block and has to be approved.

5.10. Proper lighting to be provided during the work, if required.

6. Methodology:

6.1. Approved Shop drawings are to be pasted to the walls of lift lobby area by clearly mentioning the details like where to start, pattern, grooves, measurements etc.

6.2. Lift Frame door location has to be checked w.r.t approved drawing.

6.3. The Granite/Marble shall be dry matched in the yard under day light and then cut to exact size required and numbered in sequence and laid at site exactly in the same order.

6.4. Button mark to be established w.r.t FFL for flooring and any sloping profile in flooring to be considered and should be given in the button mark. (Ref Fig-1).

6.5. Lift sill level must be 10 mm more than FFL of corridor flooring and gentle slope has to be given from lift sill to lobby area. (Ref Fig-2).

6.6. Laying of mortar mix (CM 1:6 or as specified) at the base of marble/granite Flooring. (Ref Fig-3).

6.7. White Cement slurry at 2 kg/ Sq m to be laid on the mortar uniformly and raking to be done to ensure bonding. (Ref Fig 4 & 5).

6.8. While laying of flooring, proper tamping with wooden mallet has to be ensured to remove the entrapped air. (Ref Fig 6).

6.9. Paper joints are to be provided in the flooring.

6.10. Curing has to be done for 3 days and checking for slopes has to be done.

6.11. Hollowness check to be done and damages found if any has to be replaced with new ones.

6.12. Check for uniform level, pattern dimensions & angles as per drawing.

6.13. Check for marble polishing for specified number of coats. (Ref Fig 7).

6.14. Check for Joints to be filled with approved color grout. (Ref Fig 8).

6.15. Check for Suitable resin compound of approved make is applied over slabs where surface is scratched.

6.16. Proper protection of flooring to be ensured after completion of work.

6.17. Checklist format to be filled prior, during and the post completion of flooring work.

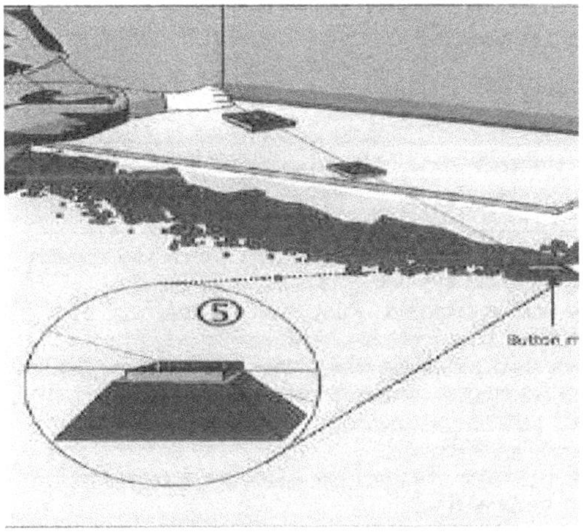

Fig-1

Fig-2

Fig-3

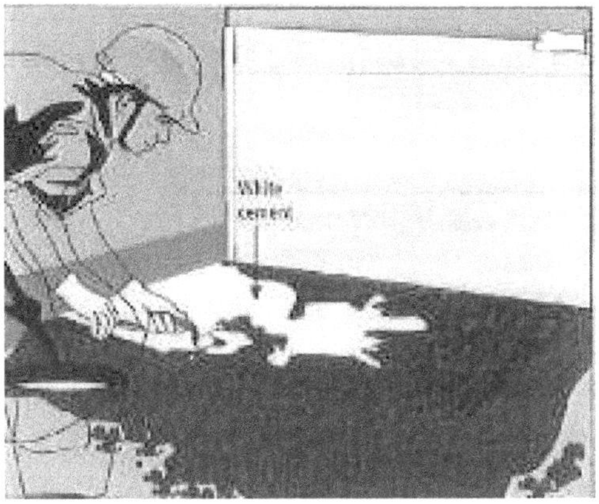

Fig-4

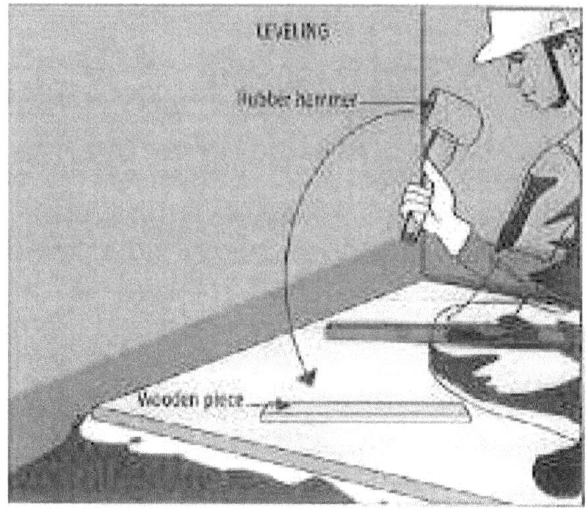

Fig-5 **Fig-6**

Fig-7 **Fig-8**

7. Quality Control & Quality Assurance:

7.1. Ensure approved Quality checklist is available before start of granite marble flooring.

7.2. Granite / Marble should be conforming to relevant standards.

7.3. Ensure Granite / Marble type & pattern used is as approved.

7.4. Work policies are to be monitored and are to be strictly implemented at site.

7.5. Check for Hollowness, line, level, evenness, joint thickness, slope etc.

7.6. Check for marble polishing for specified number of coats.

7.7. Ensure Curing has been done for 3 days.

7.8. Ensure approved grouting material has been used and manufactured and expiry dates of the material checked.

8. Safety:

8.1. Safety PPE's will be provided for workers.

8.2. First aid box will be provided at the site office and good housekeeping will be ensured.

36

METHODOLOGY FOR GRANITE / MARBLE – LIFT CLADDING

1. Scope:

- This method provides a system of control for "Granite / Marble – Lift Cladding" in order to attain compliance with the specifications and drawings.

2. Drawing Reference:

- Block Layout / Architectural Drawings/ Relevant Drawings.

3. Equipment's:

- Granite / Marble cutting machine, Trowel, Mixing pan, wooden mallet, Plumb Bob, Sprit level, Square ruler, Tube level, line-dory, Measuring tape, Polishing machine, etc. (Ref Fig 1)

4. Tradesman:

- Granite / Marble Layer / Masons & helpers.

5. Work Policy:

5.1. Cladding work shall be started only after completion of Entire Tower Block work, Plastering in Lift lobby and LMR waterproofing.

5.2. Cladding work shall be started only after Lift Frame erection of all floors including basements.

5.3. Cladding works shall be initiated only after completion of Lift lobby flooring.

5.4. Before starting of cladding work, all the MEP works should be completed including testing.

5.5. 1 m level (from FFL) marking should be done on lobby walls.

5.6. Floor level has to be established and cross checked with Lift frame fixed.

5.7. Location of Lift operators has to be checked prior to start of work.

5.8. Cleanliness of the area has to be ensured by the execution team prior to the commencement of cladding works.

5.9. Material to be checked and segregated for Approved uniform color, texture, thickness and for defects if any.

5.10. Every granite stone/granite tile should be cut to the required size and pre polished as per drawing.

5.11. Cladding Mockup has to be done for every block and has to be approved.

5.12. Proper lighting to be provided during the work, if required.

6. Methodology:

6.1. Approved shop drawings are to be pasted to the walls of lift lobby area by clearly mentioning the details like where to start, Cladding top level, pattern, grooves, measurements, etc.

6.2. Clear door opening has to be checked w.r.t to lift frame of the floor. (Ref Fig 2).

6.3. Rough Plastering should be 12mm thickness and proportion of cement mortar should be CM 1:4.

6.4. Block In charge has to ensure the wall which is to be cladded is rough plastered to true plumb, right angle and suitably cured prior to cladding.

6.5. The Granite/Marble shall be dry matched in the yard under day light and then cut to exact size required and numbered in sequence and laid at site exactly in the same order.

6.6. For slabs used for cladding, the back of slab should be pasted with rough pebbles using epoxy bonding agent to enhance surface bonding. (Ref Fig 3).

6.7. Check for Cladding stone is fixed to the wall using approved adhesive of proper thickness and checked for verticality and line.

6.8. Tamping with wooden mallet has to be ensured to remove the entrapped air. (Ref Fig 4).

6.9. Check for grooves if any provided and edges are finished as per approved. (Ref Fig 5).

6.10. Check for Chamfering, nosing and corner joints at over lapping area provided as per drawing.

6.11. Check for lift operator cutting with mechanical tools. (Ref Fig 6).

6.12. Check for uniform level, measurement, right angle of door jambs.

6.13. Curing has to be done for 3 days.

6.14. Hollowness check to be done and damages found if any has to be replaced with new ones.

6.15. Check for marble polishing for specified number of coats.

6.16. Check for Joints to be filled with approved color grout.

6.17. Check for Suitable resin compound of approved make is applied over slabs where surface is scratched.

6.18. Checklist format to be filled prior, during and the post completion of flooring work.

Fig-1

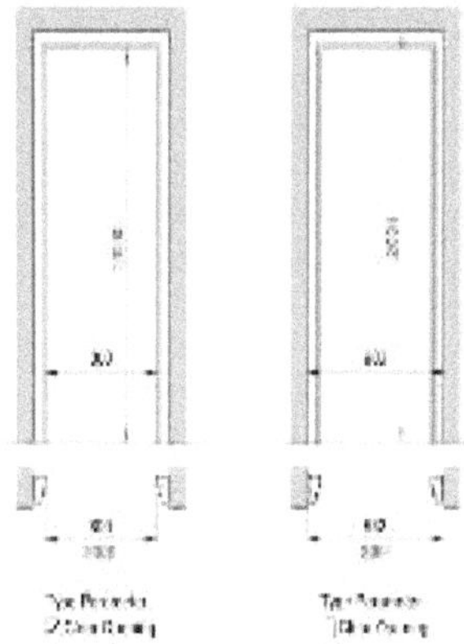

Fig-2

Fig-3

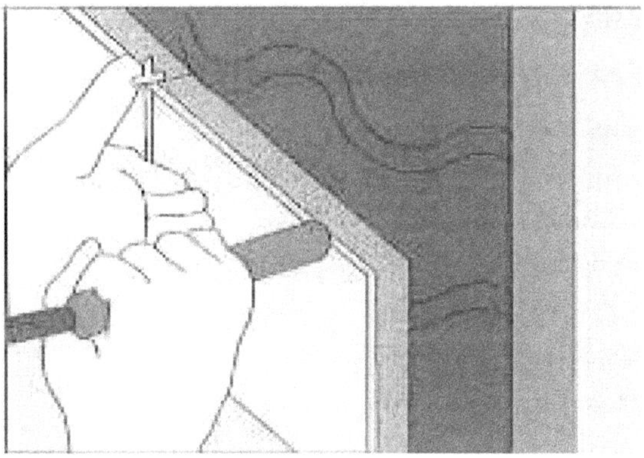

Fig-4

Fig-5

Fig-6

7. Quality Control & Quality Assurance:

7.1. Ensure approved Quality checklist is available before start of granite marble cladding.

7.2. Granite / Marble should be conforming to relevant standards.

7.3. Ensure Granite / Marble type & pattern has been used as approved.

7.4. Work policies are to be monitored and are to be strictly implemented at site.

7.5. Ensure Curing has been done for 3 days.

7.6. Check for Hollowness, line, level, plumb, evenness, joint thickness etc.

7.7. Check for marble polishing for specified number of coats.

7.8. Ensure approved grouting material has been used and manufactured and expiry dates of the material checked.

8. Safety:

8.1. Safety PPE's will be provided for workers.

8.2. First aid box will be provided at the site office and good housekeeping will be ensured.

37

METHODOLOGY FOR SWIMMING POOL WORKS

1. Scope:

- This method provides a system of control for "SWIMMING POOL WORKS" in order to achieve compliance with the specifications and drawings.

2. Drawing Reference:

- Architectural Drawings / Relevant Drawings.

3. Equipment's:

- Waterproofing tools, Stone and Tile cutting machines, Notched Trowels, Mixing machines for waterproofing materials & tile grout, Wooden mallet, Sprit level, Square ruler, Tube level, line-dory, Measuring tape etc.

4. Tradesman:

- Waterproofing masons & helpers, Stone & Tile Layers / Masons & helpers.

5. Work Policy:

5.1. Swimming pool shell including deck concrete works must be completed prior to start of services.

5.2. First pond test must be carried out after conformation of all provision of services by the swimming pool vendor. Any leakages found should be rectified.

5.3. Coping works must be started only after completion of above point 5.2.

5.4. Waterproofing works must be started only after completion of coping works by the authorized and approved vendor only.

5.5. Final pond test must be done for the pool and any leakages are to be arrested prior to start of Tiling works.

5.6. All MEP works should be completed including testing prior to tiling.

5.7. Before starting Tiling works, ensure pool MEP services, waterproofing works and all deck finishes are completed.

5.8. Detailed tile layout shop drawings should be prepared and work to be executed as per the drawings.

5.9. Stone and Tiles are to be checked and segregated for approved color, texture, dimensions and for defects if any.

5.10. Only approved adhesives and grouts are to be used for pool works and their expiry dates have to be checked.

6. Methodology:

6.1 Approved Shop drawings are to be pasted to the walls by clearly mentioning the details like stone and Tile pattern, measurements etc.

6.2 MEP clearance must be taken prior to starting coping and waterproofing works.

6.3 All penetration for fixing ladders, handrails should be completed prior to waterproofing.

6.4 All MEP works should be executed as per the approved method statement.

6.5 Approved Adhesive should be used in the coping works as per the specified thickness with notched trowel within the specified open time.

6.6 A gentle slope of 2 to 3 mm in the coping must be given towards the gutter.

6.7 Test for leakages should be conducted for 72 hours prior to start of waterproofing.

6.8 Waterproofing should be done as per the approved method statement.

6.9 Final pond test should be done prior to tiling and any leakages must be arrested.

6.10 Button marks to be established w.r.t FFL and any sloping profile in flooring to be considered and should be given in the button mark.

6.11 Only approved tile adhesive of specified thickness should be used with specified notched trowel with in the open time.

6.12 Only approved grouts are to be used for pool works.

7. Quality Control & Quality Assurance:

7.1. Ensure approved Quality checklist is available before start of swimming pool works.

7.2. Granite and Tiles should conform to relevant standards.

7.3. Ensure Granite, Tiles type & pattern used are as approved.

7.4. Ensure approved Adhesive and grouting material has been used and manufactured and expiry dates of the materials checked.

7.5. Work policies are to be monitored and are to be strictly implemented at site.

7.6. Check for Hollowness, line, level, evenness, joint thickness, slope etc.

8. Safety:

8.1. Safety PPE's will be provided for workers.

8.2. First aid box will be provided at the site office and good housekeeping will be ensured.

8.3. Area should be properly lighted, ventilated and ensure dust free environment.

38

METHODOLOGY FOR MIVAN STRUCTURE

1. Scope:

➢ This method provides a system of control for "MIVAN Structure made with Aluminium Formwork- Concrete Walls and Slabs" in order to achieve compliance with the specifications and drawings.

2. Drawing Reference:

➢ Shell Drawings / Floor Plan Drawings / Shuttering Layout Drawings / Structural Drawings / Relevant Drawings.

3. Equipment's:

➢ Total Station / Auto Level with accessories, String line, Auto Cross Laser Instrument, Measuring tape, Steel cutting & bending machine, RMC Plant, Transit Mixer, Needle Vibrator, Straight Edge.

4. Tradesman:

- Formwork foreman, Operators, Driver, Carpenters, Bar-bender, Masons & helpers.

5. Reinforcement Work for RCC Walls / Shear Walls / Core Walls:

5.1. Work Policy:

5.1.1. Structural drawings should be followed strictly for all reinforcement details of walls.

5.1.2. Bar bending schedule should be available at the site prior to start of reinforcement work, however the wall reinforcement should be checked as per structural drawings.

5.1.3. Reinforcement steel should not be shifted over to slab before survey marking.

5.1.4. Ensure usage of approved binding wire for tying reinforcement.

5.1.5. After Concerned Vendor engineer's checking of all walls in two flats, PMC/Quality Engineer inspection should be called for.

5.1.6. Wall reinforcement tying permission should not be given if no staggering of laps provided.

5.1.7. Ensure for tying of cover blocks for the reinforcement along the height prior to calling the PMC/quality engineer for inspection.

5.1.8. For electrical/services points, clearance from MEP team should be taken.

5.2. Methodology:

5.2.1. Reinforcement should be checked as per drawing for diameter of bar, spacing and lap length.

5.2.2. When bars of two different diameters are to be spliced, the lap length shall be calculated on the basis of diameter of the smaller bar.

5.2.3. Electrical points will be provided in the walls and concurrence to be taken from MEP site team.

6. Formwork(Aluminium Formwork) for RCC Walls / Shear Walls / Core Walls:

6.1. Work Policy:

6.1.1. Only approved shell drawings are to be used for setting out.

6.1.2. Reference points should be transferred from the level below using an electronic instrument with Optical plum or Laser instrument.

6.1.3. Setting out lines should be continued through openings, external corners etc. by a minimum of 150mm or as agreed

6.1.4. An offset line is to be provided from the wall location as a means of checking & to assist on the alignment of the Formwork.

6.1.5. Wall mounted working platform should be erected prior to external wall panel erection.

6.1.6. For the initial first floor setup it's necessary to prepare a Timber Kicker secured to the perimeter edge of the slab including Lift cores and Staircase areas as a means of support for the Formwork.

6.1.7. Ensure internal side of the wall panels to be erected first and then external side of the wall panels to be erected for ground floor only.

6.1.8. Ensure external side of the wall panels to be erected first and then internal side of the wall panels to be erected for above ground floor (1st floor onwards).

6.1.9. Ensure all edges and contact face of the formwork is properly cleaned and oiled prior to fixing in place.

6.1.10. It is important that Wall Ties are kept clean & in good condition & not left lying exposed on the floor slab to human traffic.

6.1.11. It's strongly emphasized use of Grease on Wall Ties is not advisable.

6.1.12. After completion of the setup, all main components need to be marked in their sequence for ease of identifying their location for installation on the next level.

6.1.13. Before striking wall Formwork ensure the following are removed:-

(a) All timber stays nailed to the concrete slab.

(b) Waller's (if any).

(c) Vertical soldiers.

(d) All pins and wedges from the panels identified for striking.

(e) Ensure all M&E fixings attached to the Formwork have been removed.

6.1.14. All Formwork components must be cleaned as soon as they are removed.

6.2. Methodology:

6.2.1. If the kicker requires adjustment for level, loosen the holding - in bolt by turning anti- clockwise, adjust kicker to the required position and retighten the bolt.

6.2.2. For the initial set up only, 50mm x 25mm timber stays can be nailed to the concrete slab or as agreed, close to the internal and external corners, to ensure wall Formwork is erected to the setting out lines.

6.2.3. Only one side of the wall panels are to be erected first. After ensuring proper alignment, positioning of reinforcement, other side formwork can be erected.

6.2.4. All Formwork begins at a corner and proceeds from there providing temporary lateral stability. A single panel at a corner will give sufficient lateral support to most walls.

6.2.5. When satisfied the corner is stable and the internal corner is positioned to the setting out lines continue erecting the Formwork to one wall.

6.2.6. Use only 2 no pins and wedges to connect the formwork at these stages the pins and wedges will have to be removed later to insert the wall ties. Alternatively, the wall ties can be positioned as the Formwork is erected.

6.2.7. Wall ties to be coated with Formwork release agent prior to being installed. Fit the wall ties through slots in the wall formwork and secure in position with pins and wedges.

6.2.8. Prior to closing the Formwork, pre-wrapped corrugated PVC sleeves are placed over the wall ties. Safeguard that they are properly located to the contact face of the Formwork on each side of the wall.

6.2.9. For ease of stripping, pin the wall panels to the internal corners with the head of the pin to the inside of the internal corner wherever possible.

6.2.10. The ends of walls and door openings should be secured in position by nailing timber stays to the concrete slab.

6.2.11. Ensure proper cover for the wall reinforcement.

6.2.12. Once the vertical Formwork is fixed in position, the external corners should be checked for plumb.

6.2.13. Formwork can be pulled by using bottle screws and chain. If the formwork requires to be pushed adjustable props can be used. This method of adjustment should only be used if necessary & kept to a minimum.

6.2.14. When deviations of external walls occur, they must be brought back to the correct plan location as quickly as possible by slightly tilting the external wall forms in one plane.

6.2.15. Walls required to be aligned by using string line or an Auto Cross Laser Instrument. The verticality of door openings also requires to be checked for plumb. Door spacers should be fitted wherever possible.

6.2.16. Steel vertical soldiers fixed in place using a tie-rod, through the cast in PVC sleeve, which will be used later for the fixing of the wall mounted scaffold brackets.

6.2.17. Kickers to be checked for alignment using a string line. A straight kicker ensures the wall on the next level is also straight.

6.2.18. <u>Wall Formwork to be stripped after 24 hours after casting of concrete.</u>

7. Formwork (Aluminum Formwork) for Slab:

7.1. Work Policy:

7.1.1. Operatives on standby should have the following equipment (at hand) (a) Pins and Wedges.

(b) Adjustable props. (c) Masonry nails.

(d) Joinery saw and hammers.

(e) A few lengths of timber for additional bracing, (if required).

7.1.2. Before fixing in position the soffit lengths (SL) and soffit corners (SC) should be coated on the contact face plus the top and bottom rails with a release agent.

7.1.3. Ensure form oil has been applied to side rails of the Deck beam prior to fixing.

7.1.4. All components should be cleaned with scrapers and wire brushes as soon as they are struck. Wire brush to be used on side rails only & Scrapers on contact face.

7.2. Methodology:

7.2.1. When connecting the soffit lengths and soffit corners to the vertical formwork, the pins should be inserted from the top preventing the possibility of the pin dislodging & falling out during concreting.

7.2.2. After fixing of the soffit lengths the deck panels can be pinned at the corners again ensuring oil has been applied to the edges only.

7.2.3. The deck beams to support the deck formwork, can be assembled on the concrete slab as per the deck layout drawing, components are held together by pinning 2no BB 350 (Beam Bars) through two adjoining beams with the Deck Prop Head located between using the 132mm pin.

7.2.4. Using the prop lengths lift the Deck beam into position. The beam is held in place by inserting a pin from the Deck beam, through the end of the deck panel already fixed to the corner.

7.2.5. The first panel in a row has to be pinned to the soffit length and the deck beam. The second panel should be pinned to the first deck panel only, (two pins are sufficient).

7.2.6. Ensuring the second panel is not fixed to the deck beam will leave sufficient movement in the beam to place the third panel of that row. Fix the third panel to the second panel, and then pin the second panel to the Deck beam. Place the remaining panels in the row using the same method.

7.2.7. A number of rows can be fixed simultaneously. The face of the Deck panels on completion can be oiled prior to the placing of the slab reinforcement.

7.2.8. On the completion of fitting the Deck panels a survey team is required to check the level of all soffit formwork and adjust Props if required.

7.2.9. Ensure kickers are properly cleaned and oiled prior to fixing in position. To prevent the pin being dislodged during concreting, pins should be inserted in a downward direction through the bottom rail of the kicker and top rail of the wall panel.

7.2.10. Where the end of two kickers meets, a B.K.S. (strap across the top of the kickers) to be fixed, ensures the 2no adjoining components will be flush.

7.2.11. Kicker level survey must be conducted on the top of the kicker.

7.2.12. <u>Slab soffit formwork shall be dismantled after 48 hours of casting.</u>

7.2.13. Ensure all M & E fixings have been removed.

7.2.14. For the removal of deck beam, remove the 132mm pin and the beam bars from the beam which has been identified for removal.

7.2.15. This is followed by removing the pins and wedges from the Deck panels adjacent to the Deck beam to be removed. The Deck beam can now be taken out.

7.2.16. Where there is no Deck beam support and the panels span from wall to wall, the soffit lengths are to be removed. Pins and wedges only to be removed on the identified component that is to be struck.

7.2.17. Care is necessary when removing each & every component from the soffit of the slab by ensuring it does not accidently drop to floor level otherwise damage of equipment will occur.

7.2.18. Props can be removed by rotating the coupler.

8. Reinforcement Work for Slab:

8.1. Work Policy:

8.1.1. Structural drawings should be followed strictly for all reinforcement details of slabs.

8.1.2. Bar bending schedule should be available at site prior to start of reinforcement work, however the slab reinforcement will be checked as per structural drawings.

8.1.3. Ensure usage of approved binding wire for tying reinforcement.

8.1.4. After 2 tier checking of slab in two flats, PMC's inspection should be called for.

8.1.5. Ensure for tying of cover blocks for the reinforcement prior to calling the PMC/quality engineer for inspection.

8.2. Methodology:

8.2.1. Check reinforcement for size, spacing, location, numbers, lap length and ties as per drawings and bar bending schedule.

8.2.2. Cover to be checked for the slab bottom and sides.

8.2.3. Chairs of 12mm diameter to be provided adequately for slab.

8.2.4. No personnel movement should be allowed on the reinforcement, if required planks, floor plates are to be provided as walkways.

9. Concrete Work for RCC Walls / Shear Walls / Core Walls:

9.1. Work Policy:

9.1.1. For walls self-compacting concrete (SCC) should be used as per approved concrete mix design.

9.1.2. Flow ability (Slump-flow test), incoming timings, type & grade of concrete and temperature checks for the concrete should be done at site QC lab.

9.1.3. Contractor's Engineer should order for correct grade of concrete as per drawing.

9.1.4. Water should not be added to concrete for increasing workability.

9.1.5. If segregated/bleeding concrete mix is observed at site, pour must be stopped and information should be given to the concerned RMC/QC person for taking necessary action.

9.1.6. Post pour check should be done for the walls.

9.1.7. Walls plumb deviation should not be more than 3mm per 3m height.

9.1.8. Check for Deviation survey [verticality checking of the structure for every 5 floors].

9.1.9. Severe honeycomb with steel exposure should be treated with approved method statement from consultant.

9.2. Methodology:

9.2.1. Minimum of two operatives should be on standby during concreting, to cover both sides of each & every wall being cast.

9.2.2. During concreting, the ideal position is slightly in front of the pour, checking pins, wedges and wall ties as the pour is in progress.

9.2.3. During the concreting, uniform level of concrete has to be maintained in all the walls throughout the pour.

9.2.4. All (Internal & External Wall) Wall Ties must be removed on the following day after placement of the concrete and external wall tie holes packing should be done before removal of working platform.

9.2.5. As the wall panels are being removed, removal of the sleeves can commence.80% of the sleeves to be removed the following day (Day 1) after placement of concrete with the balance 20% removed by 10am (Day 2) and are to be removed using long nose pinch pliers.

9.2.6. Post pour concrete should be checked for verticality with lower floor.

10. Concrete Work for Slab:

10.1. Work Policy:

10.1.1. For slabs normal/conventional concrete should be used as per approved concrete mix design.

10.1.2. Proper lighting to be provided for night work. For slab concreting, barricading should be provided at sides.

10.1.3. Slump test, incoming timings, type & grade of concrete and temperature checks for the concrete should be done at site QC lab.

10.1.4. Contractor's Engineer should order for correct grade of concrete as per drawing.

10.1.5. Water should not be added to concrete for increasing workability.

10.1.6. For inspected and approved walls & slabs, concreting should be done on the same day, if not done inspection should be done again.

10.1.7. Post pour check should be done for slabs.

10.1.8. All construction joints to be identified and clearance to be taken before casting.

10.1.9. For slab top level up to ± 6mm level to be allowed.

10.2. Methodology:

10.2.1. Prior to concreting 16mm diameter M.S bolt is fixed to the kicker (with a 26mm x 16.5m vertical slotted hole) always located tight to the bottom of the slot. This bolt remains fixed to the casted concrete with a flat washer and nut to act as anchor. After concreting the slotted hole allows for an adjustment if required for improvement on the level of the kicker also controlling the verticality of the Formwork.

10.2.2. Initially walls should be casted with self-compacting concrete and slabs should be casted with normal concrete as per specified grade.

10.2.3. The sunken areas should be casted first and the others areas are to be casted after completion of the sunken areas.

10.2.4. Concrete should be compacted properly by using needle vibrator.

10.2.5. The Concrete should not be stacked beyond a height of 300 mm at any place.

10.2.6. Things to look for during concreting are

(a) Possible movement of Pins/Wedges due to vibration.

(b) Beam/Deck props adjacent to drop areas slipping due to vibration. (c) Ensure all bracing at special areas stays intact.

(d) Overspill of concrete at window openings etc.

10.2.7. Broom finish should be done over the slab surface.

10.2.8. Special care must be taken at the lift shafts by ensuring kicker levels and levels of concrete surface.

10.2.9. Concrete level survey must be conducted. Concrete up to + 6 mm is acceptable and above 6 mm must be chipped to correct level. Slab surface should be marked with paint indicating a plus (+) or minus (-) as the survey is being conducted.

11. Quality Control & Quality Assurance:

11.1. Ensure approved Quality checklist is available before start of MIVAN works.

11.2. Cement, Fine Aggregates, Coarse Aggregates, Water, Mineral Admixtures& Chemical Admixtures should be conformed to relevant standards. Ensure approved mix design& proper grade of concrete has been used.

11.3. SCC mix tests (Flow ability: Slump-flow test, Viscosity: V-funnel test, Passing ability test: L- box test) should be conducted as required at site QC lab before dispatching concrete to site.

11.4. Steel should be conformed to relevant standards.

11.5. Work policies are to be monitored and are to be strictly implemented at site.

11.6. Sampling of concrete for compressive strength & workability should be done.

11.7. Ensure the compressive strength of concrete cubes for 18 hours (SCC), 36/48 hours (Normal), 7 days & 28 days has been achieved as specified.

11.8. Ensure for level survey and ensure concrete levels within +/- 6 mm.

11.9. Ensure door spacers have been fitted.

11.10. Ensure for Kicker alignment has been done by using a string line.

11.11. Ensure Wall Formwork has been stripped after 24 hours after casting of concrete.

11.12. Ensure Slab soffit Formwork has been dismantled after 48 hours of casting.

12. Safety:

12.1. Safety PPE's will be provided for workers.

12.2. First aid box will be provided at the site office.

12.3. Safety nets should be provided for periphery of building for immediate two floors.

39

METHODOLOGY FOR GYPSUM PLASTERING WORKS (MIVAN STRUCTURE)

1. Scope:

- This method provides a system of control for "Gypsum Plastering Work on Concrete Walls (Internal) and Ceilings" in order to achieve compliance with the specifications and drawings.

2. Drawing Reference:

- Floor Plan Drawings.

3. Equipment's:

- Trowel, Plastic Bucket, Plumb Bob, Aluminum Straight edge, sprit level, Square ruler, Tube level, line-dory, etc.

4. Tradesman:

- Masons & helpers.

5. Work Policy:

5.1. Gypsum plaster must be started only after completion of water testing of above floors and completion of structure minimum three floors above.

5.2. All debris shall be removed and cleaned for centerline marking.

5.3. Before starting of plastering, all the wall tie holes, DSR holes, honeycombs and any extra openings should be closed with approved non-shrink grout and cured enough.

5.4. Pond test must be completed for the ceiling / roof slab prior to the start of Gypsum plaster

5.5. In case of any leakages observed, waterproofing must be done and ensure watertight ceiling

5.6. Water jet test must be done from the outside for the wall tie hole packing and rectification must be done if there is any leakage. Ensure water tight walls prior to Gypsum plaster.

5.7. All ledge walls in rooms must be completed including C.M. plastering prior to start of Gypsum plaster

5.8. Bull Marking to be done for wall & ceiling at a time. If any chipping is required permission from PMC/Quality Engineer to be obtained as all the services has to be coordinated

5.9. Bull marks for minimum of one entire flat to be done before calling the PMC/Quality Engineer for checking. Ceiling plaster and wall plaster to be done preferably by same mason and should happen simultaneously to avoid the undulations in the corners.

5.10. MEP clearance must be taken prior to plastering.

5.11. Electrical switch boxes must be filled with thermocol prior to plastering.

5.12. Wall and ceiling surfaces should be properly hacked or approved bonding agent must be used

5.13. Top floor plastering to be done only after completion of terrace water proofing.

5.14. All wall conduits / pipes should be closed with non-shrink screed and fiber mesh and properly cured before start of plaster for walls and in coordination of services like electrical and plumbing.

5.15. Gypsum plaster/ putty should not be applied at dado portions of kitchen, wash basin & utility.

5.16. Clean the surface from dirt, dust, grease, loose particles etc. and approved make of gypsum has to be applied for interior walls & ceiling and approved coarse putty must be applied for utility, sit out, corridor and staircase areas.

5.17. Electrical junction boxes must be kept open and should be closed prior to 1st coat painting

5.18. If plastering has gone up to 3rdfloor, ensure that post plastering checklists must be closed in the lower floors.

5.19. Walls with undulations / plumb out above 12 mm should be done with C.M plastering as a leveling course and Gypsum plaster to be applied over and above C.M. plastering.

5.20. Termination of ends at openings should be done only after fixing of UPVC windows and door frames.

5.21. Mockup has to be done for every block and has to be approved.

5.22. Skirting top gypsum finishing should be done only after surface is dry to true level and line as per approved mock up.

5.23. Proper lighting to be provided during the work, if required.

5.24. Gypsum bags stacking in flats should be not more than 4 bags height.

6. Methodology:

6.1. Centre line / Reference line should be taken from the corridor and line perpendicular to the center line has to be taken into the flats.

6.2. Centre line and offset line for each room shall be marked and Bull marking shall be done with reference to this offset line.

6.3. Sufficient bull marks should be made available

6.4. All the bulged portions should be chipped off in line with the gypsum bull marks.

6.5. Fiber mesh should be fixed rigidly at all the electrical & plumbing grooves over the screed

6.6. Ensure that 1 meter level markings are made available on all walls.

6.7. Bonding agent should be mixed thoroughly prior to uniform application over internal walls & ceilings.

6.8. Gypsum plaster should be completed within 3 days of bonding agent application or as per manufacturer's recommendation.

6.9. Water should be added to the Gypsum powder as per the manufacturer specification and prepared gypsum plaster mix should be consumed within the initial setting time as given by the manufacturer.

6.10. Undulations in plastered walls to be checked with aluminum straight edge and line- dory. Same should be rectified immediately while the plaster is in fresh state.

6.11. Spilled plaster on Electrical junction boxes, on walls & floor should be cleared on the same day of work.

6.12. All door and window openings after plastering should be checked by templates as per specification.

6.13. Day to day plaster work waste/dead material shall be removed and proper housekeeping to be maintained at site.

6.14. Gypsum plastered surface should be air cured for 3 days.

6.15. Hollow sound test should be conducted on plastered surfaces to ensure proper bonding between walls and plaster.

7. Quality Control & Quality Assurance:

7.1. Ensure approved Quality checklist is available before start of Gypsum plastering for MIVAN walls.

7.2. Gypsum Plaster Material should be conforming to relevant standard.

7.3. Work policies are to be monitored and are to be strictly implemented at site.

7.4. Ensure centre line / reference line has been taken from the corridor and line perpendicular to the center line has been taken into the flats.

7.5. Ensure water & gypsum powder ratio maintained as per the manufacturer specification and prepared gypsum plaster mix has been consumed within the initial setting time as per the manufacturer specification.

7.6. Check for all door and window openings after plastering by templates.

7.7. Check for line, plumb, right angle & dimensions.

8. Safety:

8.1. Safety PPE's will be provided for workers.

8.2. First aid box will be provided at the site office and good housekeeping will be ensured.

40

METHODOLOGY FOR INTERNAL PAINTING WORK (MIVAN STRUCTURE)

1. Scope:

- This method provides a system of control for "Internal Painting Work (MIVAN Concrete Structure) - Internal Walls and Ceilings" in order to achieve compliance with the specifications and drawings.

2. Drawing Reference:

- Architectural Drawings / Relevant Drawings.

3. Equipment's:

- Finishing Trowel, Aluminium Straight Edge, Sand paper, Roller / Brush, etc.

4. Tradesman:

- Punning Masons, Painters & helpers.

5. Work Policy:

5.1. Internal gypsum plastering including coarse putty for sit-out, utility &corridors, UPVC window frames fixing must be completed earlier to 1st coat putty/skim coat application.

5.2. All the snag points should be attended before 1st coat putty application.

5.3. Cracks are to be properly treated prior to application of 1st coat putty.

5.4. Tiling work must be completed prior to 2nd coat putty.

5.5. UPVC windows shutter fixing& tiling check lists must be closed prior to primer application.

5.6. Doors must be fixed prior to 1st coat paint (We need to check this during sample work and decide).

5.7. Tile skirting top& door hardware must be protected.

5.8. All MEP testing, tile grouting, Electrical, CP & sanitary fittings should be completed before second coat of paint.

5.9. Proper lighting to be provided during the work, if required.

5.10. Mockup has to be done for every block and has to be approved.

6. Methodology:

6.1. POP punning to be done in between tile dado and false ceiling in toilets and a groove of 8 mm x 4 mm to be provided in the punning above dado.

6.2. After 2nd coat putty, surface must be kept ready for primer by sand papering and proper cleaning with cloth.

6.3. Light checking must be done for surface undulations and are to be rectified before primer application.

6.4. Application of primer & emulsion paint on walls & ceilings should be done by using roller and corners should be finished by using brush.

6.5. Application of primer must be done as per the manufacturer specification.

6.6. All touch up works and surface undulations if any observed in light checking (after primer) are to be rectified for perfect line and level wherever required before 1st coat paint.

6.7. Apply 1st coat of emulsion paint as per the manufacturer specification.

6.8. Apply second coat of emulsion paint as per the manufacturer specification.

7. Quality Control & Quality Assurance:

7.1. Ensure approved Quality checklist is available before start of painting for MIVAN walls

7.2. Ensure POP, putty & primer has been used as approved.

7.3. Ensure paint brand, type & colour has been used as specified / approved.

7.4. Work policies are to be monitored and are to be strictly implemented at site.

7.5. Light checking to be done for surface undulations.

7.6. Ensure uniform application of primer & paint on the internal walls & ceilings as per manufacturer specification.

8. Safety:

8.1. Safety PPE's will be provided for workers.

8.2. First aid box will be provided at the site office and good housekeeping will be ensured.

8.3. Proper platform to be made for wall height and ceiling.

www.ingramcontent.com/pod-product-compliance
Ingram Content Group UK Ltd.
Pitfield, Milton Keynes, MK11 3LW, UK
UKHW061304190726
13845UKWH00038B/1269

9 789362 612977